Godfreys Wheelbarrow - A letter from Africa

Written by Padraic Dempsey, Edited by Patricia Fors

Copyright © 2016 Padraic Dempsey

ISBN-13: 978-1506147178

ISBN-10: 1506147178

Godfreys Wheelbarrow – A letter from Africa

DEDICATION

Dedicated to the children of Nkwawangya school on the foothills of Kilimanjaro, to our fearless leader Godfrey, and to the love of my life – Patricia.

ACKNOWLEDGEMENTS

A few fearless friends and my fantastic fiancé.

To my good friend Susanne – whose ideas about climbing Kebnekaise in Sweden eventually led me to Kilimanjaro in Africa.

To my brother JJ – who mentioned briefly climbing Kilimanjaro one late evening after a party in Ireland some years ago.

To the gang who stayed in our home at the rainforest village – what a team.

To Violet – whose morning greetings and smiles will forever remain with me.

To Godfrey the warmest and kindest man in all of Tanzania.

To any of you I may have met on my journey either through the countless flights and travels that led me to really believe that the world is a small place. To those I met during the 100's of kilometers of hiking that led me to mountains, and to those best friends from around the world always supporting my various quests and adventures.

Finally, to my girl – Patricia – whose daily text messages gave me so much hope and inspiration and were so welcomed. Your spirited presence while I was in Africa warmed my heart in the darker moments and shone like a thousand guiding stars against the silhouette of Kilimanjaro – daily welcoming our future. Love of my life, for all of my life.

THE STORY

This book was written first as a letter to my then friend Patricia. It was mostly written during my stay in Tanzania during July of 2014 while I was working as a volunteer for the Madventurer group. Halfway through the adventure in Tanzania, we decided to turn the letter into this book that you now hold. I hope you enjoy it.

Padraic

June 2016

Introduction

Early 2014 I got a connection request in social media from a guy named Padraic. I didn't know him personally but had heard several times about his brilliance in his work. Working with human resources made me build a huge network. Always valuable with networks, always in chase for great talent and exchange of new learnings, when accepting his invitation, I was not aware that I just opened a door to a great story. It took several months before we met. After working on an academy approach for my employer, and announcing the success in social media, one evening, in early May 2014, Padraic invited me to a working dinner. After working a bit too much, as usual, I was tired and did not really feel like going to a social event but in the last minute I decided to go. I became immediately impressed by this great business mind with similar thinking as mine about leadership, business and also life. This guy had a story to tell, a story of life experiences so different to many others.

So it began, a story of exchanging life events and long discussions of values and beliefs. This book came to life as a letter, a very long letter written daily from a volunteer in Africa telling about his daily experiences and reflections. Reading Padraic's letter made me realize that this was not a usual letter, but a letter from a person going through life changing moments. Touched by the story he described, I suggested to him halfway through his trip that this material should be turned into a book. And this is the result you finally hold now in your hands.

This book is a mixture of his adventures as a volunteer, his feelings while being in the third world as well his deep dive into his mind over life, beliefs and difficult experiences throughout his life. Padraic describes how it is to be a volunteer but also reflects the reality the local people are living in. It is a description of sadness and joy, a reflection on poverty as well as also cultural richness. Thoughts of our world as well as of the people who don´t know anything about our world and the appreciation of life they enjoy and share far from our materialistic lives in what we call the civilized world.

The happiness of togetherness and sharing among all the people, no matter how little they have, compared to the chase of meaning in life in our western world when we already own the world. Or do we own the world? How should we increase our society's awareness and compassion as well as learn from this, the importance of human values and beliefs which gradually are eroding in our society?

This book is suitable for everyone curious of what it means to be a volunteer, to read more about the third world and how we can contribute as well as what to expect if you choose to go on this journey yourself. This is also a reflection of a psychological journey of a person coming from a difficult background in the poverty of Ireland. It gives us a historical, cultural and religious perspective of what was happing on Padraic's side of the world early 1970´s to 1990´s. It also shows what life events made him to go the way he did. The letter and later the book made me both find tears as well as find myself laughing at hilarious stories of life adventures. Besides the seriousness and deep insight, the book is full of humor and good laughs from Padraic's travels during his rich and adventurous working life.

Finally, this book is for all of you who just want to take a break and experience a real love story unfolding as it came to life through two people exchanging beliefs and values of our world and our lives. Sharing sad and happy experiences and who found themselves as best friends and in the end life partners. Everything growing through a letter while being 10 000 km apart...

Patricia Fors

June 2016

Background

1975

It's June.

It's raining.

Shite, (Irish slang)

It's another workday.

The strawberries are plentiful but the plants are wet. Wish it would rain more, so we could go home. Eddie Kelly asks us all to be careful, don't miss any, they will go moldy... Would love to go home... Wish mother would come soon, with some warm tea and buns. Wish I could keep up with Pauline (sister), she earns the most. She is 11. I am 4. Mother comes, teatime at last....

After we finish it is time to fix the cows and calves with father, my favorite work, spending time with him and laughing a lot. Of course it was hard to shovel shit and grind turnips and carry bales of hay, but the cows and calves were happy... All 4 of us kids worked on the farm in some shape or form. Kate drove the tractor – badly – but it moved, wish I could do that... when she was young she ate soil, maybe that's why father lets her drive, maybe she is nuts after all.

1976

Early May

Today was history – father asked me to drive the tractor. Would have loved to write that it went well, would have loved to write that I now know how to drive it. What I can write is that I should learn to turn at the right moment. Father told me to go slow so that he could keep up throwing the cowshit out the back of the trailer connected to the tractor. He told me to go straight – so I did. All the way. Now when you get to the end, I learned after, then the steering wheel becomes an important object. It should be rotated in one direction so that one doesn't end up down the feckin' ditch... hhhmmm this important little uninteresting piece of information I seemed to have missed in my 30-second instruction from father... SHITE. So day 1 driving wasn't the best moment for little 5-year-old me.

(Note to self – learn to start and stop the vehicle and ask if there are possible difficult tasks or challenges to master along the way when the vehicle is moving)

Once I got it, I was fathers tractor man... we worked from dawn to dusk, the best school – the fields, the cows, the calves, the hardship, the laughter and tears – we could have it all daily...

1979

November/December

Margaret Thatcher clamps down on school reforms in UK. Not really of interest for an 8-year-old Irish kid unless you connect it to the fact that a psychedelic band called Pink Floyd have a song just then containing lines '...we don't need no education...' From an LP called 'The Wall', this rightly pissed Maggie off as 'Top of the Pops' declare this the number 1 single for Christmas 1979.... Did we really need no education? – Grand, lets skip school and go work on the farm... excellent.

David Bowie sang about Kooks – (it is one of my sister's favorite David Bowie songs) - 'if the homework brings you down, then we'll throw it on the fire and take the car downtown' – yes – if all these people are into it (skipping school) and making money while doing so then who needs school?

1980

Sometime during year

Dave Fanning – Irish Radio God – plays a band called U2… from an LP called Boy… 'We are a band from Dublin, Ireland, this is our first single – we hope you'll like it….' And then starts 'Out of Control' WOW what a noise – wild, no control – is that allowed? Is it possible – can I be out of control, what does that look like? I am 9. In third class – my teacher Miss Mary Kelly thinks I am good at mathematics; my second cousin Pauline calls me professor because I know all the answers.

I like U2, Pink Floyd, JJ (brother) loves David Bowie, we know all his stuff 'cos JJ is older so he chooses the cassettes tapes we listen to every night on Pauline's old Philips cassette player. My favorite David Bowie song is Aladdin Sane – it felt like he was singing 'a lad insane..'

1984

The U2 gang have a new album 'The Unforgettable Fire' they have a song called 'Bad' – how on earth could that be any good? Irish athlete John Treacy wins a silver medal in the Olympic marathon and Carl Lewis wins most of the golds that can be won. At this stage I worked full time part time (as in all days from school) on Jim Kehoe's farm, I'd moved from Eddie Kelly's a few years back… more money but tough conditions – I liked Jim though, he treated me well…

1984 Christmas

Band Aid

Bob Geldof and a street gang made up of Bono/Midge Ure/Sting and whole lot of others gang up on the world and produce the song 'Do they know it's Christmas' – number 1 for weeks and the world is made aware that Ethiopia is dying of hunger. We were often hungry at home, who sings for us? No-one. We just work and pray each Sunday for the poor of the world, Band Aid is huge.

1985

July 13th

London

Geldof had a dream, a drive, a desire and a passion – he also had the ear of many. The Boomtown Rat pulled off, at that time, the greatest show on earth. His 'leap of faith' led to Bono's, and Bono's led to mine.

Late afternoon at Wembley stadium – U2 arrive on stage...

'We are an Irish Band. We come from Dublin City, Ireland. Like all cities, it has its good, it has its bad, this is a song called Bad', Bono starts with a few lines from Lou Reed's 'Satellite of love, hhhmmm', then comes 'Bad'.

'If you twist and turn away, if you tear yourself in two again'...

Watching Bono turn this moment into my destiny stills gives me the goosebumps. At what should be near the end of the song he jumps into the crowd, connecting to the world – which he had said he always wanted to do… he would later describe this moment in the 1986 book 'The Unforgettable Fire' as his 'leap of faith'. I was 15 when I read that book and fully in tune with what Bono meant – you have to find it, something to dive into, something to chase, someone to look up to, a hero. As Mathew McConaughty says in his Oscar winning speech of 2014… (for Dallas Buyers Club (great movie)) … what would my 'leap of faith' be and when would it happen… I had a million questions in 1986, U2 did their Conspiracy of Hope tour as well as played Maggies Farm at Irelands Self Aid show that year… 'I ain't gonna work on Maggies farm no more…' My own world started to change. I had to get out, I had to go to Africa, I was sure it was meant to be.

2005

Live 8.

Geldof gets his gang together and pulls of another great show – Make Poverty History was the theme, to end extreme poverty – I was married with 4 kids… the greatest show on earth grew up and took place all over the world – not to be missed, the greatest message on earth – not to be missed – of course I would be there making poverty history…. No doubts, questions or resistance, I joined **www.one.org** to start getting involved.

U2 and Paul McCartney kick off Live 8 and Pink Floyd end it… the world is a beautiful place.

Geldof once more holds his hand up and tells us again 'I don't like Mondays' and '…the lesson today is how to die…' appropriate for what the subject was.

During the show they showed a video showing a girl 10 minutes from death in 1985, then Geldof brings her on stage alive here in

2005, her name is Birhan Woldu (check her out - a hero in her home country now) ... 'He who saves one life'. Geldof is God.

Another heart breaking video story showed a mother boiling stones in front of her kids telling them that they would soon be ready for eating, the kids slept with no food. Everyone left the euphoria of the show for a few minutes as Geldof pronounces – 'this is why we are here'.

U2 team up with Pearl Jam and create UJam – for a concert in Hawaii, they sang 'Keep on rocking in the free world' Neil Young's classic anthem. Fantastic.

2011

July

While on holidays in Ireland I went to the Irish Aid office on O'Connell St. in Dublin. Here I found out that there were certain conditions for my travel to Africa. Examples were to have a certain amount of money in the bank, a job to come home to, a permanent address etc... and all I felt was that it's never gonna happen – I will need another lifetime. Damn it, too old, too settled, fuck – I hate this. TV shows with galas for this and that all making money for the poor in Africa, I don't want to give money (not that I can't) I just want to give me. To give my all and just for a while to see if I can... why can't I? Seems everywhere I turn it's not going to happen – shite.

2012

September.

Met and spent some time with Susanne, a friend of mine for many years. We talked about climbing and hiking as we hiked through south Sweden. We discussed Kebnekaise (highest mountain in Sweden) and decided to climb it. Susanne also decides that she wants to move to Germany... she does soon after – Kebnekaise – yes – someday – in other words – most likely never.

I had spent many great weeks and weekends hiking in Sweden and other countries either alone or with friends and really enjoyed those times. Now I need mountains, there is a great sense of accomplishment completing a 90km hike in 5 days or a tough Alpine day climb – it's a wonderful feeling and also great fresh air for the soul. The mountain cleanses very many thoughts and helps focus...I love it.

2013

July – climb Kebnekaise – highest in Sweden and Ben Nevis – highest in UK.

August – climb Carrantwohill – highest in Ireland

While in Ireland in 2013 I met up with my sisters Kate and Pauline and brother JJ. We discuss the climbing etc. and JJ tells of his fascination with mountains and in particular Kilimanjaro and Everest – if only one day it would be possible.... We discussed and drank – a lot, it was a good holiday.

Later that year in Hamburg I met Susanne and her boyfriend Simon and we get talking about mountains and Kilimanjaro came up. We said we would climb it together in 2 years – when I would be 45...

YES – of course – we agreed - while not particularly sober I might add.

Become Facebook friends with Patricia Fors near the end of 2013 – I saw that she will work with a training academy, we share some messages and agree to meet sometime to discuss – cool.

2014

February

Was just checking out some details about planned a trip for 2 weeks to Ireland – dates – boat costs – etc. Then I decided to just look at the Kilimanjaro possibilities, after all in just 2 years we should be going…. Why not be prepared. The company called Kilroy travel are one of the potential operators so I check them out.

On this page I found something I couldn't believe…. Or maybe I was just too lazy to have researched.

For years, since 1985-1986, I had wanted this opportunity to go to Africa and do some volunteer work in some way, shape or form, a dream far beyond me I was sure. A dream that I wouldn't achieve so it slept as I chased others and did well, but Africa haunted me… and there it was, right in front of me. IT JUST HAD TO BE DONE.

What will it be like? What about the food? The colors?

The smells, the sights, the sounds of this entire world as it's spinning around. Very excited by the idea. I threw away all thoughts of travelling to Ireland that summer, I was going to Africa.

2014

May/June

I had met Patricia a few times briefly for coffee and dinner, we chatted daily or sent messages; we were becoming friends – very easily. We enjoyed each other's company. I did not know what it would be like in Africa, I told her all I felt about it, and it felt good to share that. We spoke of life values, of our experiences, of our doubts and fears. We became closer quickly.

These letter I wrote to Patricia turned into a mix of stories of feelings and incidents, adventures and challenges, all mixed with the various poems of those days. I sometimes look forward already to getting to the end of an adventure in order to look back and reflect in it. Or maybe I will never get to that end and for sure there will be more adventures.

"After nourishment, shelter and companionship, stories are the things we need most in the world." -

This is my Africa dream story

July 3rd 2014

This evening I am so excited that sleep will just have to wait, there is too much in my head to prepare, to execute, to dream of, another checklist, another control of already controlled passport and yellow fever documents...tick tock.... Visa photos needed, home insurance stuff, etc. etc. people to inform that I'm alive when I arrive.... Books I want to write, poems, stories – a lifetime adventure waiting just around the corner ... and it is happening later today... tick tock.... After living in Sweden for nearly 20 years, the normal comforts I knew of would now become quite varied over these coming weeks... I feel full of expectation. I just want to feel as much as I can feel and let go of all things at 'home' and maybe, just maybe, find myself a new home, at peace at last with my haunting dream.

A poem to begin with….

Would you believe it is possible?

To make a reality of the impossible

Would you see yourself take a chance?

To ask a beauty to dance

Would you see the light of tomorrow?

In the eyes of a complete stranger

Would you dance the dance of a thousand dreamers?

In a silhouette of colliding stars

I see the reflection in the eyes of beauty

Once they had hidden dreams

I see desire in a beating heart

Warming to a new dawning sun

I see ambition to dream out loud

To escape conventions limiting shroud

I see within these moments

The beauty of this - our great world

<u>And so it begins….</u>

July 3rd leave from Copenhagen for Amsterdam then on to Nairobi, then the final leg to Kilimanjaro airport. The flight from Copenhagen is like any other of the 1000's I've done… BUT taking off for Nairobi really felt special – next time on land – that's gonna be something special – the dream comes true…. Dreaming aloud all those years ago – and here I am – on the way to Tanzania, through Kenya.

I wonder so much about what I will see, feel and experience there, I have been lucky to have been around the world a few times but this is something more special. The last time I felt like this was when I went to China the first time; it was a long time ago now. I wonder also how it will be writing to someone in this way. Telling stories, episodes – it will be a very different way to express ideas etc… at least for me. I am sure the writers of famous letters (as Beethoven's 'Immortal beloved') felt these things too… probably.

I was thinking if it would be possible to write a page of notes every day, I remember reading that Dan Brown (Da Vinci Code etc..) wrote 3 pages a day as he created his books. I saw an interview with him once and he spoke about working from 5am each day on his books, how could he then just write 3 pages, but then again what he writes is quite a different quality to my stuff. It may be a while before I get to any best sellers list. I wonder how many books you need to sell for that?

Strange the thoughts that go through your head while in airports or on planes, leaving, arriving, people separating, people meeting – new acquaintances, experiences, so much going on in the heads of so many. I wonder often how many people are underground in metros at any given time, or in the air, it must be millions. I thought when I lived in Ireland that Dublin would be a very crowded city, people everywhere, then I went to China – wow. I wondered often how the people managed there, with simple stuff like organizing road works, health care, expanding cities etc. I wonder what I will see in Tanzania and how I will compare it to everything else I have been lucky enough to see. I wonder what will happen if I were to get sick, or get a toothache – that would be a nightmare, I should have seen dentist a few weeks ago, and I hope I do not live to regret that, as I did in China once.

That time when I arrived there (in Nanjing, China) and I had a terrible toothache, it was killing me for all of the flight over. I arrived in Nanjing at 6am and as usual went straight to the factory, I asked Ellen (our Q manager there) if someone could take me to the dentist - No – we don't have those, but you can go to the tooth doctor instead at the hospital. So off we go. Since I was a VIP there (never knew why) we went straight through the ER and upstairs to the top floor.

When I walked in all I could see was a line of legs sticking out from ends of beds, this looked very scary to me. Ellen had sent a girl with me to help translate (my Chinese wasn't the best). We meet the doctor and he had a look in my mouth and asked how long I will stay, 2 weeks (the usual trip length) – Ok then I could get some drugs and when home go get my tooth fixed. I wondered if the drugs would numb the pain. They did, of course, and a lot of other stuff was numb too. I took one tablet and was flying, wow, this was cool. The doctor said to take one per day and be sure to 'NOT' bring them out of China, so all was fine and we left. I was soon stoned off my head for at least 2 hours, lovely colorful times. How to deliver mgmt. training in this condition? Somehow I managed. I had 15 tablets and 12 working days and I was to take one tablet each day and when leaving I should flush the rest in the toilet, make sure to remember that.

The trip home was a bit chaotic - out of Shanghai - with some Russian dudes being very drunk and fighting on the plane, once we landed in Moscow they were arrested on-board the plane by some aggressive cops. I continued to Copenhagen. While at the baggage collecting my bag, I saw the drug dog... didn't think too much as they go around in most major airports. BUT then I remembered, in my bag I had 3 tablets 'that should be flushed in the toilet' hhmmm – I wonder will he notice – he sure did, and he went totally ballistic - not good. I was brought to an interrogation room and asked about 4 billion questions, we had embassy calls to Ireland, China and Sweden before they then just let me go with a warning. I was just happy it did not happen going into Thailand – which was my next trip, that could have been a very different outcome.

July 4th arrive Nairobi international – feels small for a capital city. While coming in I saw what Bono called scorched earth – and this was wintertime here. I had seen red clay soil/land in Morocco but that was nothing compared to this. I ate at a small café which turned out to be one of two similar sized places in the whole airport, the coffee was Americana – shite colored water... hhmmm why was I here? Ok just passing through – no worries. Leave to Kilimanjaro – do a flyby of the Kilimanjaro mountain (big one – actually the highest in Africa) – what a sight – I am so awake, alive and now far away... from Ireland, my family and friends – this is a distant place. During the flight, I thought about writing to Patricia. I thought that it may be a way to tell her about me and my life and times and maybe get to know her better... and let her know me in a different way that people usually meet. Imagine writing a letter to someone over a month. Now that just could be the way to spend evenings – it felt better than writing about work – decided. I will write her a letter, and maybe she will see some transformation during that time as I live through what is about to happen. Maybe she can see through what I write that I am someone else, a lot of 'maybes', I feel so excited about this idea. Landed at Kilimanjaro airport, interesting lack of flow at the airport – not the most efficient place, paid our $50 for visa and that was it – officially in Tanzania. No car, no comfortable bed, no rain, and no normal Swedish summer – this is a very different place. But not just any place and not just any holiday, this was about volunteering – giving from all we have and can share to those who need it most. I don't know what happens next, but I cannot wait to see what it is we will do and what we will learn while here.

July 5th we go on a hike to a waterfall at the base of Kilimanjaro – all call it 'Kili' – disrespectful I thought... anyway we see the wee hill – it's magnificent. After that we go to Reggies grandfathers place (Reggie is the guide) to see how coffee was being harvested, roasted and ground to make coffee for us – very interesting day. Later that evening we go to Zumbaland – no - not the South American dancing stuff (that I cannot do), but the local outdoor big screen place to watch world cup football and to have a wee drink or two. Louisa (our project leader) introduces us to Konyagi (local gin) and we are off – heavy party, we stay at the Kilimanjaro Backpackers hotel in Moshi – they have Wi-Fi. I wrote to Patricia and told her about what we did... good to let her know I am alive, even if hungover.

July 6th – a quiet Sunday – looked around the town – mobbed by street traders all wanting cash money, they sell so much stuff, junk, and anything else you want – how about some weed, some Bob Marley – you look like a Bob Marley guy they said to me – if only they knew my past... anyway we would leave later for the village... Anne and Adam turn up late...we leave at 445pm – that's Africana time for 2pm...

Louisa shows us the house and the school and describes the project... work will start tomorrow. We discover the long-drop toilet, interesting sight... didn't understand what a long-drop was or the need for extreme precision while going to the loo until I saw this rather small hole in the ground, better aim straight...

The kitchen was interesting. A wooden table with a basin for water. 2 pots, 1 knife and a fireplace. What more does one need?

I started to think of the letter to write to Patricia and if I would be disciplined enough to write daily. It could be a few pages by the end, I guess.

Tomorrow work begins. At last. My chance to help. *Leap of faith...*

The letter

My dear Patricia

SMILE. Thanks.

Its Monday July 7th – we sit around our table and all are writing something, it's been a great day here – so much done and so much sweat, I feel so happy knowing the body didn't break as I thought it might at times, 50kg bags of cement are very heavy you know…

As I walked to the school this morning I wondered what awaited, what an adventure this could really be. As I found out, all I felt was this is so right – a dream realized and I was so in love with it… It was really me, covered in dirt, hands bleeding from blisters, doing something good.

I wonder of what you do and how you smile and what you are up to, and if all the presentations at work go well, I am so far removed from you at this point it feels bizarre.

Food is mainly vegetarian so far. It is okay. At least we get dry food – the shelter we build will be for the kids so that they do not eat or have to walk to their dining hall in the rain. It was upsetting as the head teacher, Bella, explained that the kids eat in the rain and it rains most days – all I thought of today was giving, a smile, a helping hand, an encouraging team talk, it was so good.

The kitchen where all the food was cooked for all the kids and us volunteers, not the most environmentally safe place in the world.

The team-leader Louisa is 26yrs old and from UK, a med student – she will be a doctor in a year, Isabelle from France 49yrs, Anne 22yrs from Denmark, Jordan from Texas 23yrs, Adam 20yrs from UK and little 'old' me, 43yrs. I was called a few things today, the grand-dad, the strong man, the only grown man (Adam is tiny) ... then the kids laughed so much as they ask my age and I answered 200 and walked around like an old man.... I feel so happy – if I died today I would be smiling. Not planning that though as there is a great autumn ahead of us. There is so much to grasp and as evenings seems quite quiet then it's a great time to reflect on what is important in these coming times ahead.

Spending great time with just great people and growing something from nothing, with great people around me... this is the start of my real adventure.

I talked to Louisa, so if I want to run a project as project leader this trip qualifies me to do that, this is just the first of many adventures... so happy... I hope I will feel this for the remaining time – all are upbeat and happy, but all physically tired – all take photos so there will be many to show when I am back... it's a wonderful place and a very basic camp. This evening the shower was a bucket of water .... That's it. I will show you. So much to tell from this already... I will focus on writing both notes and poetry to you, both encourage and enlighten me... poems will come I am sure but feel labored just now... Hakuna Matata – it means no worries. That's how it is here... don't worry about me... can't wait to tell you all from the little I have seen so far.

It's Tuesday evening. We play Uno to pass the time until the football game kicks off at 11pm, its 920pm now, I won one game and lost 4, 5 play so I guess it's even.

This morning I decided to let others go ahead with the work and I just went along with them but after about 15 minutes I was back in the strong man role. It was a heavy day until about 4pm then I saw Mount Kilimanjaro appear from the clouds – I have never seen such a sight - truly magnificent, I thought straight away of writing so much but couldn't take my eyes off it – really a majestic sight.

I thought of you a lot today – at one point I was covered in mud and cement and shite and all I was wondering was what you were wearing and if you would approve of my looks – not pretty for sure but still I felt good.

I remember when we met just before you went to Copenhagen one evening and you looked so professional, really nice…. I seldom have looked that way when we met. Today was definitely some version of worker casual.

We met the builder's kid today - Thomas. The tiniest little child I'd ever seen, out and about in the sand and dirt, continuously in our way but so very cute.

I think of my kids when at the school but also when the gang at the house ask about family, it is unusual that older people (like me) do volunteering like this. Actually it is odd for guys in general, so it's often family discussions, questions etc. interesting to get to know these great young energetic people - they have all the world ahead of them and they give so much daily.

Today the builders cut down a full tree using just machetes – they just went crazy and attacked the tree from three sides and within 5 minutes the tree fell. All I could think of was what one of those could do to a human body – we are not next door to Rwanda but still close. Soon we go out in the blackest dark to walk about 500m to the pub – actually a house with a shop in the back that doubles as a pub at night – it's so dark outside though…

In the afternoon we were about to end and the builder, Godfrey, asked the gang to make some more cement, the gang wanted to stop and asked for a team talk, I said fine, you guys go, I stay… I gained a lot in that moment of giving an extra mile. Everyone stayed. My hands are cut to pieces and bleeding, sore from blisters and cuts and legs are bruised… mood is great though, I like what we are privileged to do here.

Today's reflections were about the wondrous variety of people and how with such little means, these poor people get on. They have nothing. Your contribution was to go towards footballs and sports stuff originally but this will now be spent on tables and chairs for the kid's dining room. We have about 7000SEK and need 13000SEK more at this point. By the end of the week we will know more exactly, what is needed here in actual numbers. We will see how we do then, a couple of us decided to make up any difference to the total amount needed, regardless of what it amounts too.

Godfrey (left) and Mesere mixing cement, we would eventually learn

Already on Friday we gain 5 more team members so we will see an increase in volume of work done, this is good and we are well on track for what we want to achieve, you will see photos. Louisa has some good bar lounge relax music, like you – so it's cozy at 'home'. The home luxuries seem so far beyond me at this point. Showered again with bucket – still haven't shaved, wonder how far that will go... I may even have a beard over the weekend. Plans are all in place for a Maasai village weekend tour – we stay in the city of Moshi on Friday night – when you will get this. Then early on Saturday we go to the village and stay over until Sunday, on Saturday evening the Maasai plan to kill a goat and the men are offered to drink the blood – of course – one has to try it. We will stay in Moshi also on Sunday evening/night so we will be able to have contact then if you have time...I really hope so. The local mosque starts again and the preacher drives the team crazy, he sounds so much even from 2kms away... I still like it though, a village guide promised to bring me there once, maybe next week.

Ok – time to sign out for tonight – cannot wait to spend an evening showing you these photos and telling you of all I have seen so far even... look forward to that very much. Take care of beautiful you. I miss your daily updates and inputs, your growing challenges, your humor and always so positive thinking. As before – look forward to seeing you in a few weeks, there will be many more stories to tell I am sure... ciao.

It is now Wednesday evening – it started raining early this morning, will come back to that later – first about last night.

Adam, Isabelle and I were picked up by Godfrey at the house at 1045pm to go to the white house pub/sitting room to watch the first semi-final of the football world cup. We got to the place in about 10 minutes – totally dark outside, but could see the silhouette of the mountain – wow. Anyway once there we realized it was Germany vs Brazil – cool. The room was dark except for the TV light, a tiny TV maybe 30cm. The room was filled with some guys from our projects and their friends, so we started watching the game, Germany score – then again and again and again and again, it was 5-0 after 37 minutes then the power went – totally dark. They said the power may come back in 25-30 minutes... Nope. We felt that we should get them all a beer as they had organized the event for us. Kilimanjaro beers were bought for all (quite cheap, I might add) everyone was happy and in good mood... cool. Germany won 7-1 we heard this morning. Home at about 1230-1245 last night.... they (the locals) stayed and drank banana beer.

Back to today

I woke at 7am, raining and I knew that the schools mud roads would be very messy and heavy, I sat quietly outside the house, sad and unencouraged at 745am...thinking 'what the hell am I doing here?', I wanted to go home.

I walked in the wet grass and a little girl passed 'jambo' (hello) she said as she smiled in the rain, this is exactly why I am here. These kids have to eat out in the rain because they lack shelter – that's why I am here – to build that for them – that little girl is called Violet, aged 6yrs and an orphan to HIV... that's why I am here....as simple as that.

The day started heavy with digging and moving sand for cement, the rain eased and it got warm, it felt ok. I did a lot of robotic stuff, disengaged from the team, lifting and moving stuff, they loaded and unloaded so I was just the donkey – strong man – in the middle – suited my mood.

I thought of you in meetings and directing and making things happen, taking control as you take more and more ground and see progress being made. I so look forward to live chats and wondered what you think of now and then regarding life, work commitments and challenges, busy schedules. I felt so distant from our usual days but so lucky to see that this is a life worth living and living this way

The White House – our local pub

as they do here is not an easy life, that's for sure. I am sure I can have some real impact, what could that be though? I'm continuously wondering about the enormity of the issues here and what could one person do... there is a riot in my head about this, a rage nearly, so I put the energy into keeping the team focused and helping as much as I can. It feels good but so very little in a really big picture.

I thought also that coming to places like this should have happened 20yrs ago as these younger people now see it. The best time to sow a tree was 20yrs ago, the second best time is now... so no regrets from the past – just think of all that I have left to give... and I cannot wait. I asked Louisa about working over Christmas and New Year in Ghana – it's possible – but still I want to enjoy and experience this first, as much as possible...

My body ached a lot today, more cuts and bruises but arms get stronger and the gang acknowledges as I lift the 50kg bags of cement – they all share. I tell of days of old when I worked on the farm and we raced carrying 50kg sacks of potatoes over a distance of 100meters in mud – just to see if we could, our bosses then said we were nuts...they were probably right, I was 17.

In the afternoon – I had most of the heavy work and needed a break from the team so I ran the water round. Walking to the white house pub and collecting 30 liters of water in 2 buckets from the stream and bringing it back to the team to mix the cement (that the builders did at first, we would all learn later). I liked the water round job, as its both heavy and alone... in my daydreams I walk with you then beside me and I describe to you the mountain as it's in full view, I speak out loud (as I do that at various times) and the locals think I am mad. I do the same in airports around the world, I sing (badly) to my iPods various mixes.... (*Note to self – get more bubbly music, mine can be a bit heavy at times...*). The mountain is magnificent. I imagine you there telling me stories about your past, present and wondrous future, about the chaos in your head, the plans to save the world. I daydream about meeting you again – I miss you and your smiles and attitude.

After work we walked to a waterfall about 5kms away, everyone was happy to finish at 4pm, Godfrey showed us the way, he walks as my father did, arms down by his side, a very cool calm dude. All the way to waterfall we could see amazing views of the hill; it is just so magnificent. The way down to the waterfall was dangerous, slopes and wet soil, we saw many people coming up with stuff like rice, banana skins for cows etc. on their heads – madness I thought. It was treacherous to walk there, never mind carrying stuff. We got back for dinner just before dark at 645pm, ate really good food, then I had a bucket shower, now its games time for a few - Yatzy and Uno, some others write and communicate with home...

The team changes after today – this constellation will never be like this again, on Friday some Germans come and the team will be rebuilt – might try some team dynamics on them – just for the fun, to see what happens – none of them are over 19yrs old – just kids...

All plans are in place for the weekend Maasai trip as well as watching the football world cup final at Zumbaland... historic occasions both, we will walk to the bus after work on Friday to go to Moshi city... its a 2,5km hike there to the bus then an hour to town (30kms in total distance). Friday night we will probably just have some drinks out in town – local beers – nice. Saturday we leave. Excited now.

Her name is Violet – that's why I am here, cannot get her smile out of my head.

Ok that's it for today, just got your sms – thanks – it's uplifting to know you are there and somehow here – I look forward to all those hours and talks... take care.

Goodnight, sweet dreams.

Thursday – today was different – easier – less stress – a lot of breaks but still we did a lot at the project, good efficient teamwork and good delegation led to balanced work – sound like a lean guy now. Today the gang asked a lot regarding 6Sigma. It was nice to explain that I teach company improvement experts and their leaders in these tools and the mind-set around the business of quality in companies that most people don't get actually. Later in day Anne (Danish girl) was delegating according to execution principles and averages etc. – cool, everyone except Jordan approved, as she carried least... ☺.

Just to explain briefly what 6Sigma is – it's a broadly used term for a group of improvement methodologies invented by both Motorola and GE. It has evolved over time to be the most successful improvement methodology ever invented, it focuses mainly on reducing variation in processes. There are some different roles in expertise from White belt to Master Black Belt, I became a Black Belt in 2004 and a Master Black Belt in 2006. In 2007 I became also a Lean Master Black Belt – (Lean is another improvement method used mainly for reducing waste in processes).

It sounded like a lot of theory when I explained it to the gang, so they were curious about practical application. So here is a real story regarding 6Sigma that I told the gang today.

The F test.

If you were a 6Sigma student you would recognize this test – but it's not what is meant here. I worked for a company that bought beds from a factory in Poland. During a visit there, we assembled one bed; it was a single bed with a pull out bed under the main bed. This pull out bed was on wheels. When we had assembled it – we pulled out the bed from underneath, I started moving it with my foot, just back and forward, and when I did this a wheel fell off. The factory manager went crazy shouting – what the hell are you doing? – I just answered by asking who are the customers of these beds? He said teenagers most likely. Fine I said, now what if teenagers are interested to have sex in this bed...and a wheel falls off in the middle of the act... this would be a safety issue... and depending on the type of sex maybe a very painful experience for them. The manager went nuts. I told a colleague that we need to report this to headquarters and stop production due to safety issues... we went back to headquarters and mentioned this to our management team. We stopped the factory and they (our management) also went crazy as a result... from laughter. I told them that we would introduce a test in our stores to simulate the situation, we already had tests showing how well chairs held up for 1,000,000 sit-downs. We decided to call the bed test the 'F' test... meaning Fuck test... It became a running joke for years there. 'Padraic introduces F test to stores' – world news... I am sure we would have got worldwide publicity if the test method had been developed and introduced at the stores... I wonder how the simulation would look, maybe we could get some young volunteers at weekends to do a John Lennon/Yoko Ono type 'bed in'... the gang fell around laughing – it was a funny moment.

While at work today when I thought of you doing your work presentations - I looked forward to seeing your sms and then it came – I am so happy this presentation worked well for you. It's like the culmination of travels, late nights and professional application of right methods – well done, so very well done.

We were able to finish at 4pm - we had done well all day to get ahead of the builders, and we all wanted and deserved to go home by that time. It's amazing how often and how much you can sweat in a day....

The carpenters came today – about a week earlier than planned as we were ahead of time, it will be messy next week as we have six more people and we cannot see what work is left to do.... We did very well. I was again called 'the strong guy' as Leonard (the builder's heavy duty guy) didn't match me for work today again – cool. But it was bloody heavy and sore as the wheelbarrows nails cut my leg badly, needed some medical treatment, good that Louisa is a med student. We saw the mountain briefly about lunchtime, it's an inspiration always, making the heavy work easier.

After work, we played badminton for a while until Anne lost the shuttlecock. I lifted Adam on my shoulders to find it but he couldn't. Some kid may find it in 10 years from now and wonder 'what the f*** is that?' I wonder how you say that in Swahili? We do our bit to enlighten. As we continued to play the locals stopped to watch as this was new to them – they thought we were bonkers I am very sure. We all showered and washed clothes, we have new guests at 7am tomorrow – they will arrive to a clothes line full of underwear... how nice for them. We all change rooms then too. After dinner – we listened to U2 and Sinead O'Connor – my music of course... just because no-one else's Bluetooth worked. We then played Uno, we had a competition and during this we had visits from a lizard and a huge spider that set the girls off, I killed the spider and the lizard got away. We told Anne that the lizard would sleep in her bed... we are sure she will not sleep. A few vodkas were had and all laughed a lot – good fun.

Now it's 2130, sitting alone... just sent you last night's (Thursday) poem (as I think/hope you read this on Friday night...) I wonder how we will view this writing in some months, I often think of that with my poetry as if they (the poems) have a shelf life. I have some very old stuff from 20+ years ago – you will see, it's very dark stuff as a lot was written while under the influence of dark clouds that haunted me for a long time, but these clouds made me. They maybe were beneficial after all, I have a lot to tell you... and I like that a lot... still didn't shave, haven't seen a mirror since I left – getting hairy and itchy now.

Today's sms was about your success and you succeeded so well, feel proud of you. I hope that some mails tomorrow include some interesting work issues but I look forward to yours most... I hope all is well with you. When I am working and carrying these blocks or wheelbarrows I just wonder what is happening at your end and what adventure you just started and what you are thinking of, your travels, adventures, concerts, traditions, cultures, visions, dreams etc...... Very curious about you.

One thing I have done nearly as a tradition by now I guess is to be outside Sweden for my birthdays. I have been away from home every birthday since 2003, in 12 different countries. Starting in Ireland in 2003, when I studied 6Sigma there, in 2004 it was a work trip to Austria then Germany in 2005. We had a great week in Canada in 2006 followed by China and Mexico in 2007 and 2008. By 2009 it was becoming a habit so once I was able to plan work trips myself I decided to try to manage this habit so it could continue. In 2009 and 2010 Turkey and Slovakia, that was the end of the work trips. After that I was planning myself and got to Cyprus and Morocco in 2011 and 2012, was in France with Pauline in 2013 and then Italy in 2014. I hope to keep up this as long as possible. Of course there will be work restraints at some point but it will be fun.

The only 2 countries in Europe I haven't been to are Estonia and Slovenia... so I need to at least get there in the next few years...

I like to wonder about you as I am very curious, so there may be some questions, hope you have the time and interest to share - hope that's ok... Goodnight XX

It is now Friday morning – all woke early to very heavy rain, no-one wanted to go to work. Myself and Adam went anyway after we had changed rooms and made place for five new people, one guy and four girls. Once at work we started digging trenches but the rain got too heavy so I decided that we should stop, all agreed of course, it gets dangerous in rain with shovels and pickaxes flying – the dangers of work. I am sure some Swedish health and safety officers might have issues with the work safety environment here. We dug two trenches while the school kids took away the small plants we had dug up. What was noticeable about the kids was that none had jackets or even coats and they all carried Machetes – all were clothed just as they were in the sun yesterday. All work stopped and now we are all at home, myself and Adam are damp – he practices Swahili with the others. Too many countries have tried to teach me a few words but I still don't get it too easily... wonder what Polish I will learn from you... I did a lot of work in Poland over many years, hope we see it together sometime...

Speaking of the dangers of work – they are slightly different from those I have seen over the years in different places. The stories of corruption here in local government give reminders of the former Eastern bloc. Have you been often in the Eastern bloc countries? I worked in Poland a lot but also in Russia, Lithuania, Czech Republic, Slovakia, Hungary, Serbia, Albania... – here are a couple of more 'work' related stories from these places.

We were working at a factory outside Moscow. I had some training sessions there and a supplier to us asked us to visit his factory... of course. When we arrived, we discussed business and factory developments with the management team and they had an armed security guard - there for my protection. We walked through the factory and afterwards I told the manager they were crap and we would never do business with them. He said he wanted 20million € worth of business... he would get none. As I informed him of this, he shook my hand and said 'goodbye, we won't meet again'. He smiled at the guard and told him to organize a separate car for me to the airport, as I deserved special treatment. As I got into the car, my colleagues said goodbye and said to me to call when I was safe at the airport, I didn't understand why, until I called them. When I did, they said they were sure I won't be there, 'no-one says no to these guys'... I did... ooooppppssss.... Still I made it home.

A similar experience from the Ukraine.

We arrived in the small town called Beregovo just past the Hungarian border after driving from Hungary and earlier Austria – a long day. On our way there (through Hungary) we passed through a small village called Hell. We were told when leaving Austria that when you get to Hell, 'just turn left', so we did – we went to a different type of hell then....

Anyway once we got to the hotel we are greeted by the hotel manager and he told us that he always shows the new guys around the outside of the hotel. We drop our gear in our room and go with him...

It was an old hotel from the communist 1950's era and in one corner, there was a Cinderella type tower with a metal roof on it, a very poor looking construction... I asked him about this and he said that it had been a normal bedroom up until recently, when a guy was killed there through an explosion. We asked who it was and all he answered was that it was some poor guy coming here to try to optimize a factory close-by... then he asks what our work was about.... We decide not to tell him as that's exactly what we did... we had no issues that trip regarding this but the hotel felt cold and scary at times. On the day we left my colleague realized he had forgotten his wedding ring when he had showered at the hotel. He realized too late and decided not to go back to get it, we felt it would be safer to not go back, word had spread about our work we reckoned. Other trips to Ukraine have more stories – again autumn chats.

Anyway back to Africa (sorry for continuous diverging) – the plan changed for today as the gang that were to be here working with us today, were delayed from Frankfurt so they come tonight instead. If it is so that the rain continues as all hope just now (even me) then we will leave at 2pm for Moshi and that means Wi-Fi access earlier – nice. So hopefully you will see this not too late this evening, it takes a while to get to town.

Our cook isn't here just now so there is no hot water and therefore no coffee... damn it. We will have smoky water instead; he boils water so that it's safe to drink but over an open fire so it turns smoky – making us even more thirsty. That's how it is.

Now it's all talk about travels and bartering and dealing with marketeers in Moshi – interesting stories all around, everyone has made a deal somewhere, that's for sure.

We discuss evening dinners and all want meat... it's been a vegetarian week so far... all also want a few drinks as well as Wi-Fi time...

I really wanted to call you last night but the coverage was poor to nothing so most calls, even local ones, didn't work. Hopefully over weekend I will have some decent coverage.

I dreamt of moving last night, look forward to it very much, deciding colors – moods etc. really liked that when I moved to my current place in Karlskrona. I think you will like some of my stuff... saw some nice and very brilliantly painted paintings that would be really nice on a white wall... really colorful and lively, most include both Mount Kilimanjaro and Maasai warriors.

Finally, back in Moshi – what a ride to town, we stopped work after 5hrs in the rain and had to walk 2,5kms to bus... the bus took 1,5hrs... so I dumped my gear in my room and rushed to get connected... nice to be here at last, city is bubbling and all is well....

So this is the end of the first week. It's been great as well as heavy – felt so good to lay on a bed and off the floor.

I hope you enjoy these notes and my apologies for their length.

I miss you and enjoy your very much looked forward to daily messages of support and encouragement.

Smile once more – just for me – thanks

Another poem just stopped by.

When the world opens it arms

And I try to see its light

I try to imagine freedom

For all things in sight

When the worlds light goes out

And the nights breathe cools my face

I try to imagine peace

For any soul in need

When the dawn comes and dreams rest

And I try to bring them to reality

I try to imagine success

So that peace and freedom reign

My soul is alive with crossed wires

Some of hope, some of desire

The worlds open arms devour us

And lift us to the heaven we once dreamt of

All that is needed is to see it

To feel it, to consume it

It's all there if we want it

Sweet freedom

It's Saturday 2200... so very tired. Last night it was very nice to have some meat for dinner at last, we had steak. Unfortunately, we got the tough end of Africana time. It will take 30 minutes + 30 + 30 + 15... so 1hr and 45minutes after we had ordered, the food turned up. Everyone was now both tired and, having drank real beer for first time in a week, also quite rowdy (noisy) we were eleven people after all. Just after we got the food then it was closing time so we had to eat fast and then run out, messy. Anyway a few of us went to the neighboring hotel where we also were kicked out at closing time but we were allowed at least to bring a beer... nice, so back at our own hotel it was card playing and singing happy birthdays to unknown people etc. – good times.

This morning was heavy, we should have met up with a few of the gang at 730 to go buy a birthday cake but this didn't happen until 8, and we were to leave for Maasai village at 9. I took 2 of the gang, Adam and Anne, to the bank, to the supermarket and to the coffee shop to order cake and we were back in 30 minutes, they were impressed that I knew the places already.

All eleven of us left at 9 to drive what they said was 45minutes, we got to the camp at 1130... the dirt roads and total lack of direction left us stuck a few times. When we got there though – wow – what a place, so bleak so open, a scorched landscape that went on for miles and miles, so fantastic to see.

The kids at the Maasai village fascinated by us Europeans – many had never seen 'our kind' before

Once we had arrived, the elders met to see what we were allowed to do and see. When this was decided and we were informed, then off we went exploring, asking questions and just observing.

First we saw the day-to-day living of the tribe, how they crafted, how they cooked and washed etc. – there is a level lower than basic. Material life has no meaning here, very few have anything and most have nothing. All the people, children as well as adults, smile as if they are the happiest in the world – amazing to see.

After this short introduction and quick tour, we heard a girl cry from a nearby group of houses so we went to see.

This beautiful girl was 18 and the elders had decided that today she should leave the village to her husband in a different village. She would not return for at least 2 years, she found out today that tonight she would marry a man she never had met. She would lose her virginity and be exchanged for a goat and a cow. This beautiful young woman was so sad, she cried out loudly as she said goodbye to all the women and children. She would not see the men before she left in a jeep, it was heart wrenching. Since her father was an elder she wouldn't get to say goodbye to him either, we all felt so bad for her, but this is their land, law, right, justice... whatever we think means nothing here.

After this, it was the elder's honor to slaughter a goat for us and fix a barbeque over an open fire. On the drive earlier the guide said I looked the bravest so I could kill the goat if I wanted, awoke some bad memories in my head but I will tell you later. I would have killed the goat if I had been asked to, I knew that.

It didn't happen that way. A herder led the goat out of the village and himself and another guy held it calmly and slowly they slowed the flow of blood to the head of the goat so it nearly fell asleep. They showed great respect and the killing moment, although graceful and calm, it still turned a few stomachs. I had seen this before and done it also in my teen years so it was just a reminder of those times, will tell you all... of course. After the goat died they skinned it, the skin would be used for beds and all of the goat would be eaten. The blood of the goat is said to give strength – so of course I tried it, very metallic... warm too as it came from throat to mug to me. A Maasai guy drank straight from the neck of the goat, some people had to turn away, and it looked quite messy too.

Anyway once skinned and barbequed we all ate piece by piece, legs, fillet, liver etc. – all went well.

The girl in the white head dress (near the tree) was about to leave...

We left the village at 3pm and headed for a local swimming area (a hot spring). I didn't feel like diving in so I talked with some locals as the team all washed and splashed. I was surprised at myself because I usually like those things but just not today. We drove back and were at the hotel at 7pm... dinner at nice Indian place at 730pm and now its 1030pm and all are so tired from sun, I look like a lobster – very red... will turn to tan I am sure.

Irish people are not too good in the sun. I come from a country where you need 3 weeks in the sun to just get white, we are usually blue from cold... so sun and us Paddies are not a good combination.

Goat – soon time to eat

Speaking of lobster and suntan... we had a working team a few years back that had regular meetings in Florida, very cool we thought. One time, in May of 2007, we had such a gathering and there was a heatwave. At least it felt like that for me, any temperature over 15 degrees Celsius is a heatwave for me, (those Irish roots).

We were there from Friday to Sunday, I was planning on teaching in Denmark on the following Tuesday. On Saturday, we were being all cool and 'Baywatch' like, we bought cheap surfboards at a garage sale, and off we went to the beach. A nice warm day. I had factor 2 million sun cream on me, surely nothing would happen to little me. After a few drinks and a few rounds of total surfing failure then this cream wore off, no-one tells me these things. After my miserable surfing moments, I lay sunbathing. Not a good idea especially when I fell asleep for an hour just around lunchtime... heavy sun concentration time... lovely. When I woke up the lobster has arisen, I am sure people on the beach were dazzled by the vision of me. I knew I was badly burnt. We went to Ron Jon's surf shop and got the heaviest medical stuff known to man, it gave some relief but I could hardly walk. By Sunday evening, I was already losing skin on my face and since I had no hair (my head was shaved usually) my head was dry too... I was teaching on Tuesday, hoping to recover and have a new face by then. Nope – that didn't happen. Flying to Copenhagen from Orlando was a nightmare for other passengers as an emerging Hellraiser (scary movie) was evolving during the flight. I felt like I looked like a leper from biblical times, with pieces continuously falling off of me, very cool indeed, quite far from the Baywatch ideal.

I landed and drove 4 hours to Skive in Denmark, I arrived at 8am on Tuesday morning just in time to start my course and then it happened. All the skin decided to fall off my face at the same moment as I stood in reception shaking hands with the management team. The most embarrassing moment in my life... and I was teaching for 3 days, leaving bits of skin everywhere. So there you go, sunshine holidays and me – not a good combination, so don't go getting ideas of bringing me off on sunny trips, unless you would like to see the leper beneath once more.

Anyway back to Africa - Today I felt on a high about seeing you soon again, just 3 weeks and I will be on my way home. Even though these will be full weeks too we will be a different team and that will change some things. So happy too about idea/possibility of going to Paris together during autumn, really look forward to that, thank you for saying yes to going... I wasn't sure you would, it was a spontaneous question even though I thought a lot about asking you, I look forward already. This evening just before we left I saw your mail from last night, thanks for your comments on my writing – I am happy you like my style... many don't as its too direct they say... I shouldn't use swear words either – according to my publisher – that's a very long story too. With all of today's barbequing and time spent in the bus, we got to talk about so much stuff. When they talked about killing the goat, I told the story of killing a cow once, not pretty... still though an element of stuff I saw growing up.

'I saw it done on a horse once....' – movie quote - I saw the movie 'Robin Hood Prince of Thieves' in 1991, while I was working in the Isle of Man, it is a brilliant movie. Morgan Freeman plays Azeem, a Moor. At one point he has to make a caesarean section on Little Johns wife and as he goes into the tent to do this, he tells Robin that he saw it done on a horse once - so of course it was possible, all went well for Little Johns wife. A few weeks ago on TV I saw a show and heard a line where one actor said to another that after watching ER once he could then perform brain surgery. It reminded me of a story from many years ago on Jim Kehoe's farm, but before that story, one from our own farm from a few years before. One Monday morning during springtime, when I was about 10, father came in from the fields to tell us that a young cow had fallen into a ditch and had her calf. The tiny calf was dead and the cow was unable to stand up. We all helped to lift the young cow and finally got her up into a box behind our tractor. Father drove her away to a warm shed but not before he told me to bury the dead calf. I hadn't done that before, so I picked it up and brought it to a special place and dug the hole and buried her. I cried all the time. The cow had been paralyzed and was unable to stand. I spent hours with her over the coming days, she cried a lot and I massaged her face and dried her tears... after a few days she was able to slowly stand and then a few days later she walked again – good, it was her first calf so she was sad for quite a while.

A few years later, there was a similar incident with a young cow at Kehoe's farm, where I worked part time. In this case the cow had tried to have her calf and slipped and broke her leg. The owner Frank, Jims brother, didn't know what to do, he called us and we all came to see and the cow was in terrible pain but couldn't get her calf out... we all just stood there. I was afraid to watch and see her as she groaned to death in agony. Frank and Jim knew she would die if nothing was done. I took a knife and cut her stomach open and pulled out the calf, then I just cut and cut into her until I cut something close to her heart and she just dropped her head in mud. The calf was alive at least... Jim and Frank just stared at me... I was shaking... but at least we had a calf... OK. That evening at dinner no-one talked – all were shocked, including me. I fed the calf milk from another cow before I went home, cycling late in the dark, all I thought of was the baby calf and seeing him in the morning again, I was glad that at least he lived. I went home and told father the story.... he remembered and told of many of his old stories for me that night, I felt happy.

The next day I woke early and cycled the 6kms to the farm, it was still dark when I got there, I had intended to sit with the calf an hour before the other workers came, to feed him and take care of him. It didn't turn out that way. When I got to the shed the calf was dead, he had got pneumonia and died, most likely because he didn't get his mother's milk the day before. I was so sad, I just held him and told him stories, by the time the others came I had fallen asleep with the dead calf across my legs... the guys asked when they woke me if I had been there all night, I wished I had been, but no. I was sad and had to bury that calf too. On reflection there was a lot of heavy times growing up... hadn't really thought of that at the time, maybe it builds or makes me think a certain way, I am not sure. I just know I am very grateful for the great days as I know that there are often dark days too.

As you can see there are a lot of things to discuss when I am back, God, I miss you. How I wish you were here in front of me now...

Goodnight – many hugs – off to bed soon, its 1 am, midnight where you are, catch you tomorrow.

Sunday

Just chatted a while in mid-afternoon with you before you set out to family evening. Sounds like you were busy there with new stuff on terrace – well done – how very efficient of you. I was busy for a couple of hours earlier, discussing books and structures and chapter headings – there will be some interesting results from these weeks. It is soon mid-July – the warmest time in 'not so warm' Ireland.

I remember as a child we would go to Curracloe beach in our old car. We had a car called a Morris Minor, now they would be regarded as a nostalgic antique, then they were regarded as a crock of an old car. I think the dim lights were at my mother's feet, father drove, and I remember if we drove at night the approaching cars would flash at us, I didn't know why until I learned about the dim light switch. We would go on some sunny Sundays to Curracloe beach (JJ, my brother, lives close to there now). Father never drove fast, I don't think he knew that a car could go over 40 miles per hour (64km/h) and if he ever ventured near that mother would tell him to slow down, she had no license.

She would smoke in the car, when all four of us kids were in the back seat. Father drove so slow that she could smoke 3-4 cigarettes in the time he took to get there, it was about 15 miles, (25 kms). I remember when we got to the beach literally jumping from the car gasping to get air.

That beach was very popular, it's where the opening scenes of Saving Private Ryan were filmed. JJ was there along with Spielberg and Tom Hanks... 15 seconds of fame. Speaking of fame – Kate (my sister) once shared an elevator with Justin Timberlake in Berlin...

This evening it's the world cup final at Zumbaland... we go with a gang of Germans and we are all in support of this great team, I can't wait... now though its supermarket time, will try to shave too as beard gets heavy... tonight partying until who knows when...

I look forward to watch the match, I actually remember quite a few world cup finals, going back as far as 1978 when you were born. I was 7 when Mario Kempes scored in that great final, strange what I remember at times. I remember that the final in 2010 was on the night before I went on a trip to China, I had a gang of friends over to watch it and when it was over, and the gang had left, I drove straight to Copenhagen airport... slept all the way to China.

On one of my first trips to China many years ago, I was seated in economy and in the middle seat of three in the back end of the plane. Do you know when you see someone and you hope they won't sit near you? You just feel – Please God – no... well along comes a Chinese guy surely 200 kgs in weight and of course he sits beside me, on my right side. Within a minute he was asleep, I was crushed, no, not heartbroken just physically squeezed against the armrest on my left.

I hoped no-one else would come so I could move. To my horror, this guy's brother (or very near relation) weighing at least the same, stopped at my row. All my nightmares came true, of course he sits to my left... so here I was, Padraic the sardine, squashed between too mega heavy sleeping and sweating Chinese dudes... it was going to be a great 8-hour flight. Luckily a stewardess saw this, or heard my last gasps of breath and asked if I would like to change seats... I nodded (couldn't speak). In 2 minutes I was free, and sitting in business class.... Very cool indeed.... And what a relief.

It is now Monday week 2. Today started late last night partying with the German gang at Zumbaland, good fun, liked it there. Good to see the final, memorable.

Up at 645am, showered and skipped shite breakfast, drank the horrible coffee and ate watermelon – ok. Chris the local 'go to' man (who fixes most logistical things) came and we loaded the van at 745am, some really heavy stuff. Some people bought some very heavy things to bring home but they had to come here first to the house first, so they needed to be moved too, loaded, unloaded etc.

We got to house at 9am and unloaded the van and then we who have been here a week already went to work. Louisa went through all the routines with the others, showing the luxurious shower and fabulous long-drop toilet.

It was good to get back to work, it was heavy with the wheelbarrow again, blisters came back slowly and we made good progress before lunch already. In the afternoon the new crew arrived and were all excited to help until after about 10 minutes. Then they started complaining, about the conditions, the weights, the lack of tools etc... All the similar things we had ourselves talked of just a week ago now seem so normal to us already, it is an interesting social study... I like it a lot.

We had to send passports to the municipality today so Louisa was away, there was no formal leader so I took over – all went ok, the crew had no objections and neither did the fundi (builder). At the end of the day, all were very tired and longed for home at 4pm.

Myself and 2 others stayed back to finish a section of work so we could all start in good way tomorrow... everyone worked hard for Godfrey and myself. At one point I badly cut my wrist so I had to stop a while – I hadn't noticed what had happened, but it bled a lot. I feel very tired now suddenly, need rest... catch you later.

A poem dropped by.

Shed a tear for a moment this day

It was a silent close moment, just alone

The enormity of the task

The hugeness of this escapade

Where to start or when to end

What is enough and what is really needed?

What gave us rights and rules?

What of their local ambitions?

Who is too blind to see?

Didn't feel that tear until it exploded into a rage

And all I could do is all I do

But it's so far from enough

It's overwhelming my soul

It's taking something from me

As well as giving – but so much more I gain

I want to tell you about Paris and my sister who lives there, as we go through this week I will add some details about my family if that's ok? Silly to ask, I guess, since when you read this it will be added by then anyway.

Pauline lives in Paris with her husband and 3 kids. They live in Suresnes, just on the periphery of Bois De Boulogne, famous for many things, ladies of the night, among other wondrous things and it is featured in the Da Vinci Code movie. Do you like Tom Hanks?

Suresnes is a nice place, a cute small city area, it takes me 20 minutes to cycle from her place to Arc de Triomphe so it's central enough. It is really cool to cycle around Paris.

Pauline and I were the only ones of the 4 of us kids at home who went to college, Pauline is currently teaching at a Montessori school near her home. Jean Christoph, her husband, works at a security company doing IT stuff – no real clue but it's quite advanced security stuff...you will see when we go there. Jean Christoph has a sister Caroline, and a brother Bertram. I met his sister a few times and his brother very often. I was working a lot near Berlin when he lived there and then he moved to Vienna, I met him there too, just recently actually and ate dinner with his girl and their son, Bertram is a really cool guy. Once in 1996 we had a very long and heavy drinking session together in Lille in France, where you had to drink some strong vodkas to quality into different areas of the pub, we qualified. The pub was called Red Square, I tried to find it again a couple of years ago when I worked in Lille but I couldn't locate it. Bertram designs guitars for musicians and plays very well himself too.

Pauline and Jean Christoph have 3 kids, Tristan is 18, Laura in 16 and Calista is 14, her kids adore me. This is mainly because I am the crazy uncle and always get Pauline drunk whenever we party, we get on very well. She will be very happy to see photos from here, as I am too actually as they are many and they all tell stories.

Now it's nearly 6pm, and all sit around doing 'homework' writing in tablets, notebooks, some small talk about nothing relevant, I sit listening to Leonard Cohen – Closing time, a tune from the summer of 1992. It was a very special time as it was then I was in a very downward destructive cycle. I wrote 100's of poems then – many around the idea of dying young as I had little to live for, I was drinking a lot of Jack Daniels those days too and Sambuca on Thursdays to get the party started. These poems I can read to you sometime, takes time though and some explanations. It's after dinner now and most are well fed, today it was French fries and beans, just ate a little, need to eat less to see any tummy effect, could do with drinking a few less beers too I guess. Our cook Simpo made too little food so when I went last, some nice stuff was missing – typical. Shower was so nice – bucket again, over weekend in town it was nice with a real shower and shave – well needed after 2 weeks of not shaving. Next issue will be haircut. It's been

20yrs plus now that I cut it each 2-3 weeks so 4 weeks will be a nightmare and surely very warm too, the reason for short haircut is a long story – those long autumn nights.

The new kids are all very young and innocent and cannot lift too much, putting more pressure on the rest of the team, the pains are welcome as its all beneficial to health but the weights seem heavier this week.

We plan a big weekend, we take Friday and Monday off. On Thursday night we all go to Moshi to see an African dance with buffet with over 20 dishes. I am sure it will be fun, then on Friday we are off all day before Saturday we leave for a 3-day Safari, can't wait.

I feel good about what's happening but the feelings inside vary from pity to rage. The kids we build for will soon get their tables and chairs that we ordered during these days, all will be in place before we leave, great that your contribution could be used for this, thank you so very much.

After dinner the school kids wash up outside. They walk between 2 houses where there is constantly pools of water, a simple pipe/drain would suffice – makes me angry, but they know and will fix it, but it's on a long list of things to do. Just found out now that we will paint the school also before we leave, these will be full weeks, tomorrow is a big cement day, so a heavy day for me with driving sand, collecting water, and carrying 50kgs again...

After our chatting over weekend I really wanted to see you soon, to see your place and chat a while... miss your daily messages and supporting words, look forward to share a lot. Goodnight.

Tuesday evening – the heaviest day yet, my God I am so sore, hands burning from lifting that bloody broken-non-round-wheeled-so-called-wheelbarrow. All are in good mood still though, but some heavy moments.

Today's reflection was on leadership. So few dare to take the chance of leading when a chance is given even though it's allowed, and reasonably acceptable, to just take the chance. Luckily the builders seem to like taking orders even if direction is theirs, they still want someone to lead, and guess who stepped into the breach. Have you heard of Kaizen? It's Japanese for 'change for the better' it's a way of working within Lean (*set of improvement tools, that have their roots in how Toyota was built*) and often it's run in project like form. I was running them in the companies I worked for before, I was the Kaizen leader and we even ran Kaizen leader training courses. There is a concept within Lean called Kaizen blitz or Kaizen event. I started to run some work at the school this way, very effective. It was like running a Kaizen week with 3 teams on different jobs – the only odd thing, from a kaizen point of view, is that I was doing the work as much as the others, in kaizen I just order people and stuff gets done.

Kaizen is another improvement methodology within the Lean tool kit. It is often used to describe two different things. One is that Kaizen means change for the better in Japanese, so it can describe a complete improvement program in a company. The other explanation is the idea of a Kaizen event where a team has a specific project and a limited time (a week or max 2 weeks) to complete change and deliver results. I ran over 100 Kaizen events while working with Lean and 6Sigma over the years and had some great results, and I have worked in over 40 countries worldwide, since 2003.

The famous wheelbarrow. Don't let that round looking thing at the front fool you. It should be a round circular shaped thing – called a wheel... it was actually a rather badly carved square shaped thing, making cornering at speed in mud very difficult.

Godfrey for sure had made this himself. Early on I was sure I would buy him a new wheelbarrow but we discovered a better need for any contributions. We bought tables and chairs for the schoolkids instead.

This morning started with the project leader Louisa being sick so Rachel was to take over but it fitted me better and the fundi's like me better too when I am very pushy. I got to be the fundi's nr. 2 so I was spreading the cement and trying to do it well, but for sure the room for improvement was very clear and very large.

We have had 3 guests since yesterday from a church and they go around trying to recruit us as well as the kids – they don't like hearing me swear, most others just accept it... they said twice that I was shaming God – so I didn't stop of course – so I'm sure it's hell for me. Again.

We got a new guy, Christian, he is from Denmark, a DJ, who just recently has worked 5 weeks at a festival in Bulgaria. We will see how he is as a worker tomorrow, we need some muscle, so hopefully he will benefit the team well.

Again today I drifted at times to thinking about your day, your great successes since you started at your new job and also what's to come. I haven't felt too much stress over the volume of work for this coming autumn, thought more about seeing you and us travelling to Paris together...

Another family member story. My sister Kate (Catriona) lives in Kilkenny in Ireland, she is married to Nick since 1993, they have no kids, neither work, Kate is 48 and Nick is 50... Nick worked on oil rigs for over 20yrs and has made some money through that as well as through rental of property in Ireland. Kate worked in a gambling shop for 19yrs and 11months just to not work 20yrs.

Since my mother died Kate has tried to be the one in charge regarding keeping family together... hasn't worked that well but when I get involved stuff happens – I like that. Kate worries a lot about me and my lifestyle and of course now that I am here she has a huge load on her shoulders, it's cool that she is there though. I like going home to see her, she was in Sweden when I was married but not since 2008. Soon again maybe... maybe even show her Lund.

JJ (my brother) was born on Christmas Eve in 1968, he unfairly got less Christmas presents as a result. He is married to Caroline and they have 2 kids, Jamie (called after a football player – JJ is the biggest Liverpool fan in the world) and Sofie. I am Jamie's godfather. I went to Ireland with Elias (my second oldest son) for his christening. We had a great time, during the meal after the christening I was chatting and dancing with my Irish family, they are a great gang, you will meet them if we go to Ireland sometime, and I would like to show you many places there. JJ works at Intel and is currently studying for an engineering degree in Dublin.

At the school one of the builders fell from the roof today, he was walking on a makeshift scaffolding. He fell onto clay and didn't injure himself but some wood and metal fell to very close to observing kids – it was quite dramatic. The rules for us are simple – no one leaves the ground, 'feet on the ground all the time'... good.

In the afternoon, some of the gang left us to play football with the kids so we were a few bodies short. The new crowd want to walk into the rainforest tomorrow, so I'm glad to have a couple of hours alone with you here in my pc... feel close to you through writing but so longing for evenings to chat with you 'live' on your terrace... and then Paris – very nice. Just now the food is nearly ready here so it's feeding time, catch up later.

Just off the phone to you, very nice to hear you – it is strange as you mentioned that we only met 4-5 times and spent just a few hours together chatting, laughing, eating, walking but still I feel a great closeness to you. Maybe because writing as we do and filling each other in on our days, creates a base to reflect as we write, I like this very much, very special feelings.

We spoke a lot in the team about my work last night, they asked about writing and poetry – since the group is now 14 it's like an intimate audience. They ask for background ideas etc. so I talk about these notes and how they will tell further stories.

Last night I dreamt of my kids and how they said goodbye at times, I miss them often and wonder of their lives, friends, ideals, values... I hope my move from Karlskrona to Kristianstad will make us closer, we will see how things develop. When saying goodbye there was always loss in their eyes, my oldest boys loved airplane crash investigations from a very young age so they often cried as I left. I was very sad for a number of years as I left the home to work. My job I had formed, developed and succeeded very much at but the cost was so huge... but lives change and people understand more when the facts come to the surface. My kids learn more facts about the how's and the why's and then they will understand more, it may never bring them back but they hopefully find some balance.

Jack is the oldest and he is such a great guy, he is sporty, intelligent, very passionate about being Irish. Elias is more creative and dreams a lot, we often talked about living in China, him and I together. Mica my daughter is gorgeous, she teaches dancing and is so very smart. Leon is a real joker, very funny and always up to mischief but has a great heart. All of them are kind, witty, and full of humor. I actually miss them a lot now that I think of it. I would love them to know my life now and see some of these wonderful African children, my kids would do well here and give their all I am sure.

Its Wednesday – 7am, woke before the gang except for Louisa and Rachel, Louisa jogs in her working boots, Rachel does yoga on our back porch. The other 11 share the floors on the 4 bedrooms, my room had 4 mattresses all like a jigsaw spread on the floor, it's like camping. The cook, Simpo, is here for about an hour already making pancakes for our breakfast as usual. The routine in food is also getting more stable, even though yesterday some variation occurred and we had meat mixed with rice for lunch, it wasn't beef or chicken... that's for sure.

This evening Godfrey brings the team for a walk so I will be able to spend some time alone. Adam will probably stay home too. He is 20 and even though he has been here for 10 days we spoke a lot last night alone from the team for the first, and probably, the only time. He asked about my work, my job, we talked of his ambitions after college – it was a nice chat, much like what I would love to have with my gang (kids) at home... soon, patience.

Our sitting room now is getting smaller as more arrive, there are 12 rucksacks in the corner of the room and all I could think of was how airlines manage such volumes of bags going all over the world. I bought a travel bag once that travelled a lot more than I did in its first few months, it was in Borneo, Jamaica, Senegal – places I am sure I may love to travel to also, maybe even accompanying my bag sometime.

There are also electronics devices everywhere at the house, chargers, iPods and iPads, tablets, loads of stuff that the locals here would have no clue of. It would be an interesting study to show them as they show us their daily lives too.

When we spoke about each other's 'real' world away from Africa I spoke of one company where we actually produced and even designed most of the electronic stuff we had at the house. Some were fascinated by this and it led to the story below being told, I remember at the time it seemed quite harmless that this incident happened but it could have been very serious.

In one of my jobs (within electronics) we used a term called bill of materials (BOM) – it describes what the content of a circuit board (or any product actually) should be with article names and quantities. I was doing some work out in USA and travelling with an Irish mobile phone designer between Los Angeles and Beijing. When we were waiting for check-in in LA, my colleague got a phone call. I paid no attention to the call until he got some question where the answer was 'the BOMs are in the bag, yes, all 200 of them'…. For me this all sounded logical as I had heard such conversations before. Then as I looked at my colleague, I noticed people slowly moving away from us… then the words 'drop the phone and step away from the bag' it was a uniformed guy with a significant sized gun and some other guys with also drawn guns, we were shitting on ourselves, 'is there a bomb in your bag?' 'yes' my colleague says, 'about 200 of them' and as he spoke the penny dropped and we burst out laughing, we probably shouldn't have done that. We were interrogated and all was sorted in one of those small rooms close to check-in. We made our flight, just about, but it was a very funny incident and a story for life.

The local lives here in Africa are simple and carefree it feels, even though they struggle daily to find work, gather water, just to simply exist reflects hardship. It is so very far from our world, so different from all I had expected even though I had expected some extremities compared to our western world. The actual enormity of the poverty is the heart-breaking factor, it's in these moments again I think of Violet and of Schindlers list – the fantastic movie. Near the end of that film there is a scene where Oscar is about to get into his car to escape being arrested, Stern (his fearless Jewish advisor) hands him a ring which has the words (here translated from Hebrew – because I didn't do Hebrew in school) – <u>He who saves one life saves the world entire</u>... Imagine just saving one life, or just changing one life enough to somehow save it. Tears in my eyes as I write this, what can I do for Violet, for Jessica, for Joshua, for Ludwig - all these beautiful children here? Every single one of these children are more willing than any at home to learn, to develop, to save their families or what is left of them. HIV destroys this area, with orphans all around and the extreme poverty it is causing a riot on my head... crying now... heavy times.

It's hard to imagine or write what I feel regarding these incidences and spontaneous outbursts of anger and sadness. I try to use that in work as a driving force, each pain, each lift, knowing it is a help for these kids, it makes the hurt easier I guess.

Simpo arrives with pancakes, maybe today they will not have the wildcard ingredient as they had the last few days, green peppers, weird onion type things... always a treat and surprise. The drinking water has been cooked over the fire again and tastes/smells of smoke – it makes us more and more thirsty and doesn't taste well at all. Last night we drank a liter of rum between us, like pirates we were, nice – it made some of the gang more open and others collapse.

We talked about nicknames from school and Adam told us a great story about when he had a huge early Michael Jackson afro haircut. One night he was jeered at a disco by older guys (probably 25+) and they wanted to sing into his hair as if it was a microphone. We all just cracked up laughing at this – it was the best story yet; his new nickname is Mike. Then we heard of other names – Shabnam was called squirrel, she is tiny and has a squirrel face apparently. She also told us about each person having an animal face, I was told I was a raven, fearless and angry when needed but graceful also – I didn't buy the graceful part (you will see when I attempt to dance), but definitely yesterday I was both angry and fearless. Angry when the kids would not get out of the way, and all the teachers and my gang had asked them to move, then Jordan said to me to tell them in a direct Irish way – so I simply shouted 'Go away' very loudly and they scattered immediately – everyone laughing... good fun. Then fearless as I took on the building role in the absence of two of the other guys – it could have been better, for sure.

When we write and document that we want to get to know more about each other – it fills my day with wonder about you, so much to discover and enjoy and laugh about – cannot wait. Looking forward very much. Take care... now its pancakes. Hope you have had a good evening.

Goodnight X

Wednesday evening – today was again a very heavy day, there is a tool we call it a trowel and it is used for spreading cement and plastering. I qualified to do this today. It was damn heavy as all the gang were focused on getting a certain amount of work done so that Godfrey would walk with the gang that didn't walk last week. All 14 were on one job and we sure worked hard. First 2 hours we drove 30 wheelbarrows and mixed the biggest pile of cement yet and even the builders were impressed by the work volume completed – it was a great team effort, my hands were destroyed with blisters and sores as were Anne's, she was very sore today also.

After lunch we were preparing for another pile and got that all laid by 330pm and all wanted to go home to prepare for the hike, then Godfrey says in a soft voice '5 more' only to me as usual. He says that since I am in charge I should tell all what to do. Even the teachers call me boss now. During the day a teacher was standing talking to and disturbing Godfrey while his own class was making noise and doing nothing, so I went to him asked loudly what his job was, he said 'teacher' – so I just said to him 'then go teach' he got the point in a very very clear manner and left. Soon after he was standing watching the girls load clay and they felt uncomfortable. I just shouted 'hey you' then he left, it's somehow cool and I like it of course as we orchestrate success in our project.

Its July 16th – 15yrs ago yesterday my mother died. I was 28 and became an orphan, father had died 9 years previous to her (in 1990). My relationship with my parents is the most important story and will take time. Just here though I can say that we didn't get along too well, my mother and I. After father died in 1990 we hardly spoke at all. When I was 16 I had a full time part-time job and was hardly at home, I stayed often with guys I worked with. Then once I was 17 I left home for good to go to college and stayed at home very seldom after. That's suited everyone fine... I guess even then I was a 'go it alone guy'.

My mother died of a heart attack when she was 62, she was reasonably healthy as far as we knew. She had gotten over me having Jack before I was married and was looking forward to coming to Sweden in August of 1999 to see Mica my daughter, who was 6 months when she (mother) died. She never saw Mica. On the day she died I was already at work at 6am and at 630am my ex-wife Linda called to tell me that JJ (my brother) had called and that mother was dead, she (Linda) was dead tired and could hardly talk (we had 3 kids to manage so she was often tired). I called JJ at mother's house and all was true, my god, it's over I thought (when I tell you the whole story you will know why). I mailed a few people and informed that I would be back on Monday, this was Thursday morning. I got a taxi home at 7am. When I got home to my apartment I sat at the kitchen table stunned by the news. Jack wondered why I was home and I told him that granny was now in heaven (even though I didn't believe so). I spent the day trying to find a flight to Dublin, there was none until Friday night so I went then (15yrs ago today). I arrived at her house at 1am on the 17th. Her funeral was at 10am, I didn't want to see her, and I wanted to drink whisky. At 8am the following morning all the family were gathering at mother's place, myself and JJ and Kate and Pauline all drank whisky before meeting them, they thought we were celebrating and were annoyed – I couldn't care less. During the funeral Pauline just was stuck to me, JJ was in bits – devastated as was Kate – not me. I was feeling grand. I told everyone and everyone knew that it was father who was my hero, so mother meant a lot less, so I was Pauline's rock that day. I know that these are a family breaking/dividing few lines but it is what it is and was that way – for me at least.

Wow - there is a lot to talk about. This poem below came to me now as I think of mother, you may see/understand I have had some difficulties in that department....

Mother will they take my soul

Those priests in black and nuns in blue

Look mother, there's a small plane in the sky

Could it put distance between you and I?

'You will never know hope, love or life,

No-one will ever love you' was all you told me

And so it went on for years and years

Hiding from your anger behind sorrow and tears

I was too small to know, to have control

All you did was place a brick in a growing wall

We filled the empty spaces with blood and sweat

How could you think that a wall wouldn't be built?

I was just a young boy raped of innocence

And so sore that tears couldn't run anymore,

In death, did you get what you deserve?

Is anyone there to save you?

Or maybe you are alone?

Reminds me of me - when I ran from you

I haven't stopped running - until now

Here in the stillness of Africa

I feel for the first time

I found peace, truth and hope

Maybe these things finally can exist

Maybe there is love from this African dawn

Even for me.

Something very great is coming.

Needed a break there... there are some things that are hard to write as I see them in my mind's eye as I write them.

This evening it was so nice to come back early from work and have first shower of everyone, it's just 530pm and I'm in the mood for writing, there was a lot today already.

Today again when I drifted into thinking mode I wondered of your greatest ever moments, the ones that made you 'you'. The ones where you thought would be mega moments for a lot of people including you but it didn't turn out that way. I have two I want to talk/write about. Both are connected to 6Sigma. The first was when I was awarded the Black Belt certificate at Flextronics. There is a story behind why I was allowed to train at all but the certification moment was what I wanted to write here... it was April 2004 – I was one of 140 Black Belts who had started training a year before in April 2003. The task was simple, 4 weeks of school, 2 projects and 5 Green Belts were to be trained and mentored through a project each. My projects were to bring 100,000 USD in savings and the Green Belts had to get at least 50,000 USD each in savings – all in profits so my costs and 20% of theirs had to be taken as costs also. I was one of three who delivered on time. The evening before the awarding of the certificate, we ate with the COO who flew from USA, with this award ceremony as a highlight on his tour. It was the biggest moment of my professional career. On the day of the certification all the white collars (over 200 then) gathered and I was the star that day, it was too cool. All was in English too just for me. My thanking speech was brief and was about how anything is possible with application of methods and discipline and powerful execution. I was immediately short listed for a director position; it was a good day.

During this time, I was consuming books on statistics and mgmt. and really going beyond duty at work having for the 4th year running over 1000hrs overtime... all was well in the world, except marriage.

One night, late, we were discussing what 6Sigma was, as Linda had no clue then, and I told her that all we now learned was showing how little we actually know about things. That we were in general quite useless at most things we did – this was a major nail in the marriage coffin as her interpretation was way too personal and 6Sigma to her after that was a more a disease than a cure and I had this disease badly. In 2005 our company was riding a great wave of 6Sigma success but no more Master Black Belts were needed, and I was desperate to get that role. So I applied externally for this course in Stockholm – my boss and mentor (now a close friend), agreed to pay after I told him that I would pay myself if he would not. He said that I had saved the company on many occasions so he would pay, in 2006 I was made Quality Director at the company and qualified as Master Black Belt, it was the crowning moment and would be a memory forever. The celebration this time was zero. I got home from Stockholm late that Friday and with certificate in hand I walked in the door. No-one noticed or cared, the family had turned 6Sigma into the disease that took daddy away, I went from the proudest moment to the saddest in my life in less than 2hrs, I will never forget that.

The Master Black Belt took me into a whole new forum of great people and tasks, from talking to Bill Gates from an office in Mexico to helping in solving court case inefficiencies in UK, to working in the Vietnamese jungle making IKEA baskets, a truly wonderful journey. And now here I am writing it all for you... we need time together... I hope you enjoy these notes and thoughts from down here in Africa... they start to feel very precious somehow.

Back now to the day by day stuff, a short overview of the people in the house – we are 14 now – 4 guys and 10 girls.

I spoke of the original gang earlier here is a short overview of the latest arrivals – 8 since last Sunday.

Rachel 22 from Ireland – a co-leader along with Louisa – has never worked on a building project and thinks we are all doing a great job, she is funny and has dark Irish humor. Has a mathematics degree but cannot count – should never have went to college, cool character.

Shabnam 29 from UK a teacher and just here until tomorrow – a good team spirit lifter and laughs all the time, she was in Kenya teaching last week and now builds here. She thinks we are crazy to aim for and then to achieve so much, she believes I am a good guy but very tough leader... the UK needs me.

Ciara – 17 from Germany – older sister to Chris (16 – see below) – has great difficulty talking while brushing teeth. She nearly died from laughing as we mentioned this to her while she was attempting to brush her teeth a couple of nights ago – we all laughed way too much.

Chris – 16 Ciara's little brother 185cms tall and very determined to learn, good worker but complains about conditions, always hungry so I give him a lot of my share.

Isobel – 18 from UK lives in Germany and goes to school with Ciara above. Very quiet and afraid of me as I am directing a lot at work site. In the evenings she seems to want to chat about school, work etc. like Adam did last night.

Sofia – 18 from Costa Rica, goes to school with Isobel and Ciara, hard worker, funny and very good at cards.

Break here – we got a call from the guys on the walk so we all went to a local bar to drink banana beer – yuck. Then we went to the pub next door... we met a character there called Elias M, who told us how great we were and how much he appreciated us being there – it brought it home to us all that we make a difference to the village – it was a real cool moment.

Valeria – 18 from Bulgaria – loves all music, from Guns n Roses to new wave shite. She works hard though and keeps the gang laughing with her poor English.

Christian – 25 from Denmark – came yesterday, funny guy travelling the world and this is his first stop. He is a teacher and a DJ so he now sits beside me and has random old music on – nice guy, worked hard today and was dead tired by lunchtime.

Just got your sms, so happy to hear from you and get a view of your day – want to share so much and get to know more and more of you...

Now its Uno time... sending you many hugs.

We plan to finish at 330pm tomorrow and hit town for a goodbye dinner for Adam and Shabnam, will be nice to get online and chat and send all this – so if I don't add more before then – I hope you liked this so far. I will add daily of course so it's up to date and growing. I miss you and I miss talking about all the stuff that we have done and worked with so far. I also hope that my going off on tangents about family are ok for you, they are all angles of my life – want to tell you so much as we get to know you more and more... take care. Catch you soon.

2am and once again I couldn't sleep – so I got up and am now sitting in the sitting room, writing again. Have just a tiny flashlight, there was an electricity cut, again. Hopefully the battery will last a while. I was talking earlier to Isobel from UK, we talked about an island between Ireland and England called the Isle of Man, it is actually a tax haven also, I didn't know what that meant when I lived there in 1991.

That year I was just sick of trying to get work on farms so I decided with a gang from college to go there for the summer. Most guys and girls who went there would get work in pubs and restaurants, so I thought why not, it would be a good experience. What I didn't know was that most people including my friends, had jobs before going there, I didn't know this until a couple of days before we left by boat from Dublin to Douglas. It is a 4-hour journey on the Lady of Mann ship, my first ship journey of significance. A few years later I would take a ship from Karlskrona in Sweden to Gydnia in Poland weekly for a few months – by then I was an experienced traveler - not so in 1991. I was so sick and when I arrived in Douglas I just needed a bed.

I slept in the cellar of a hotel that one of the gang had got a job in... it wasn't the most comfortable start to my trip. I had an open-ended ticket for 3 months. The next morning, I went to the government buildings to sign up that I was in the country. You were allowed to stay 10 days and if you didn't have a job by then you had to leave or else stay illegally and they had cops everywhere so that was not an option – so I had 10 days to find work. I met some of the gang and they had an apartment on Broadway, a cool middle of the beachfront city apartment. I walked the full length of Douglas seafront asking for jobs but they were all taken by the well-prepared and mostly Irish people, many from Belfast as I remember now.

After a few days of trying everywhere, a job came up in the job-center – stock manager at a clothes store – 25kms from the center of Douglas. So off I went for an interview… of course the Irish accent (and charm) helped so they would contact me, great – I told them I had just 6 days before I had to leave so I needed an answer. On day 8 after watching cricket (*and learning all the rules*) they called from the store – I could start on Monday. This was Friday… there was a boat I should be on already on Sunday but the agency said it was ok so I stayed and worked there.

It was a simple job unpacking boxes and stocking shelves – easy. We worked Monday to Wednesday and Friday to Saturday – so I basically had 2 weekends each week, one on Wednesday night and the real thing on Saturday. Cool. After some days in the job I met my second cousin – Pauline – the one who called me professor when we were in the same class in school years before. We decided to rent an apartment together and hoped to get a gang to stay with us, we had a lot of friends who wanted to stay somewhere also. We found a great apartment on Broadway and the rent was £100 per week. we had 5 bedrooms so we decided to tell 5 people that they could stay, all had to pay £25 each, myself and Pauline would take care of the landlord and the deal making. So we were seven people, I shared a room with a cool guy from Belfast – we all partied a lot.

Each Tuesday I would meet the landlord and pay him the £100, we collected £125 from our roommates the evening before, so we lived for free and made a profit – nice...

While there, we had some great storms and as we lived on the beachfront we would run across to the sea and go surfing during the storms – at the time it seemed like a great idea, now it sounds suicidal.

On the ground floor of our apartment block we had a hairdresser who only employed students. They would cut hair late into the evenings for half price. So of course me being the cheapskate I was, I went there. My first visit resulted in me nearly losing my job. The haircut was a disaster; I think the concept called 'bad hair day' originated with this student... it was a mess. The next day at work I was told to stay in the stockroom and not come out until I could have a proper haircut. That evening I got it all shaved off by the same student, she missed some bits so I took the tool and finished it myself with the use of mirrors, not a pretty sight – I was never meant to be a contortionist so bending to reach the missed bits hurt a lot, maybe yoga would help... The next day I was allowed to meet customers on the shop floor once more – even if my skinhead scared some old customers...

Eyes heavy, it is now 430am, the mosque calls believers... my mattress calls me, will try to unravel the mosquito net, feel like skipping it, the rainforest has less mosquitos than all thought, that is fine with me.

Good night, good morning, hugs... a short poem before I sleep

See the sign of you in a foreign sky

You walk through my day as thoughts fly

Wonder of the color of your dreams

And if they include time to be free

I find hope in knowing you are there

As you are here just beside me

Every day a day closer to seeing you

Every moment a thought of you floats by

The past has a lot to carry forward

As we discover the future calmly over time

It's a time worth taking

It's a time to see a new view

It's a time to smile

And think of beauty

As we hold that in our hands

XX

Thursday – Today started with rain, some hoped it would last, but it didn't – good thing too, since we would be off on Friday and Monday. We had a very clear target after today's team talk over breakfast to finish a certain section... all were helping as much as possible. I met the math's teacher and he apologized for being a lazy gobshite (*Irish slang for idiot*) and said that after he saw us working that no-one talked to him like I did so it was a positive even though uncomfortable change for him – I heard that before.

A guy in Canada once told me I was the only person ever to tell him he was crap at his job, this woke him up and he excelled later... interesting, the truth hurts at times, but is needed in leadership, being candid, as Jack Welch would say. The day went relatively fast, with great work and well-coordinated team, everyone was so pleased when we hit the target by 330pm... then up steps God Godfrey with the quiet voice – 'more' so the enthusiasm dropped dramatically ☹. Then we all just went at it and got the 'more' done quickly and we finished at 4pm. We all went back to the house and since we had packed before breakfast, we just needed to collect our gear and go.

Adam and Shabnam were leaving so they took a taxi with Louisa and we all walked to the bus. It was the second time we did this and the second closest to death by bus journey in a week, it was truly bonkers. There were 25+ people on this minibus and a small see through cage/box with 4 chickens – all pissed off to be travelling... it takes an hour and it's a slow torturous trip – you could never script it, just has to be experienced.

We got off at union café and got to showers – we took over the hotel as we do and in the space of an hour, 12 had showered and we were off in a limo to the Honey Badger resort for an evening of drink, African buffet, drumming and dancing, it was brilliant. I got to dance like a 'spastic leprechaun' (*Irish troll*) according to Rachel (*Irish – so she is forgiven*). Once the dancing stopped we were asked if we would like to try to drum on their goat skinned drums. I thought of the murdered goat from last week... so of course I went first. There was about 50 people and the drummers, all looking at me not playing well. The real drummer tried to hold my hands but it just didn't work... so he let me free – so off I go and get wild on the bongos, it was such fun, laughed so much as the locals danced to my Irish African drum – great fun. After the dancing and drumming was over we sat around and drank cocktails – heavy night ahead... we finally got back to hotel at 1am – long after planned time. Then it was round 2am, drinking and playing pool until 3am – then round 3am, off out to market to buy Konyagi gin and passion flavored Fanta... the night ended up about 5am and Adam and Shabnam went straight to bus and left... me – I went off to bed.

When I thought about your day, and since I thought it was Friday, I wondered about your weekend and what you would be up to. Then when we chatted earlier, I realized it was just Thursday, the days all melt together, I guess. I was thinking a lot about who to tell you about next so it's now time for my father – if you have the patience, it is a long story.

When I was born, my father was an old man, a small peasant farmer who married through arrangement at the age of 47, his wife was 26. They were married on November 12 1963; they went on their honeymoon when JFK was shot – they knew where they were – just like you probably know where you were when world events happened... like 9/11 for example. I was born in 1971, father was 55... too old to play football etc. so we had little of that type of time together... but when I started work at age 4 he started to help me how to think about work and money. When we started picking strawberries and potatoes – my father called it 'picking up the pennies' it never left me... so when I got to do what I do now, I keep his voice in my head, it's about picking up the pennies – saving the right money. He was and will be always in my head.

When I was aged 5 we started hunting rabbits. Each Saturday we would hunt and shoot them for dinner. Father would shoot and I would run to catch the wounded rabbit – and chop its neck – I will show you, then we would pick mushrooms, what I never knew was that these were magic mushrooms. So father would pick these and dry them out and then after 2-3 weeks he would use them as tea flavors. I was drinking this tea each week and for a few hours each Saturday I was stoned – 'stoned immaculate' as Jim Morrison would say. A colorful time... my mother never knew, as far as I know. I had some regular 'happy Saturdays'. The term 'enjoy weekend' had a different meaning back then for sure.

When I was born, father was happy that he had 2 girls and 2 boys, mother was sick of being a mother at 34. She asked the priest to talk to father so he did, and that was the end of their sex life, he was 55 and she was 34...I don't know really how much more I can write about him, I think it's easier face to face as he meant and continues to be a force in my life. I could go on and on here that's for sure.

Friday

Woke at 9am. Heavy head - like a car crash, a riot inside. This felt like I was caught in a moment of madness – drinking in Africa when all the world can see is despair – there is no way to compare. We advise the new arrivals not to compare to home, just accept it as it is... I find that hard, there is so much you feel like you want to do and contribute with but the enormity... it's hard to grasp. In many areas of my work at home I have often told people that I feel nothing, no emotions, no feelings – zero. Here I feel a lot and I feel like I am getting closer to the real me and I like that very much and I love very much that I can share that journey with you, as we get to know more and more about each other over the coming times.

I look forward to going to Paris together but most of all I look forward to seeing you in August and just chatting evenings away and we discover the ways we both think, how we can support and help each other – a lot to do.

It's now Friday afternoon about 440pm... Today was a quiet day, I ate a nice long slow breakfast with Christian, the Danish DJ, we were at Union Café – he was dying from a hangover... my riot had calmed... We had a mission – to buy him a sleeping bag... so off we go, mission clear, destination supermarket...but there nothing happening there, so no sleeping bag. Then on to the sports equipment shop, just sold out – damn it. Then across to the hiring out stuff guy... his suggestion to Christian – hire a sleeping bag for a month – cool – for the bargain price of 600$... WTF????? So the bargaining begins – it doesn't go well. He says 600$ and I say I want a 590$ discount... nope – we were slightly off balance with that starting point – this was not going to happen. We left and a guy outside asks if we are looking to buy a sleeping bag – so off we go walking a few more streets with this guy and come to his store, (I guess he got a tipoff). Anyway, once in the door, we got cornered by 3 guys pushing to sell everything to us 'tourists' – we check one bag and it's perfect for 55$... so we start at 30$ my advice to Christian was to go down if they did, nope – nothing happening there either... shite. Then the guy who brought us there says we can go somewhere else and try there so off we go again. Jaysus (Irish slang) this was becoming more work than at the school, its 30+ degrees too, so it's bloody hot for the emerging lobster. We arrive in a tiny hiring gear place and we find a bag for 50$ - we agree it's worth and Christian says fine – 'but'. Yes, after all our walking there is a 'but', the girl selling wants only to hire it out and not sell. She has to ring her sister, her mother, her cousin, her far off relative, her uncle's goat – and finally after an hour - 50$ - it's ok, Hakuna Matata – it means no worries...

After this we went back to hotel, and I wanted to write to you, so now I sit on the rooftop bar of the Hotel Maria with a beer and a smile as I think of you. You would I hope enjoy this chaos and calm as it's that mix all the time. This week my head revolved around pity and anger – words in my head for the latest days. Pity for the poverty and suffering and lack of what we call amenities – anger for the inability to do all of what's needed and how to manage that, all of this mess is the basis of my heads riot. Its creative and interesting – like doing a real life study on my ever-changing self.

Am I in a good place? – Yes, my head is clear and direction getting more and more set in my head. We need face-to-face time to get it clearer and more understood, also though some more time to get there, I look forward to all moments around getting to know you.

This evening the plan is dinner with the gang at about 7pm... but we have new arrivals also needing some inputs and drinks ... will see how it develops.

Tomorrow its safari time – we leave at 7am I think, so no late night needed... 3 days looking for lots of animals and great views, how I wish you were here, not just in spirit.

Saturday

Sane people should be asleep, its 530am, went to bed 4hrs ago and should, by now, since it's a day off, be asleep and resting – nope. The city's mosque calls again and the believers, I guess, go believe. Today will be different, as it's the first of a 3-day safari. We were told yesterday that this will bring us in close contact with the 'big five' – everyone talks about them as if they know them personally, I don't know them at all – besides elephants, lions and leopards... could always google but I will ask someone in the know, I guess, lazy me.

We leave at 730am in a safari jeep, saw it last night – very cool toy indeed – hope it's comfortable, I was discussing with a new arrival, Peder, from Stockholm last night about the bumpy roads and I must say I miss my Audi and its smoothness. We ate really good Indian food again last night – and here begins another learning session... food.

I love good food and I love hanging around in a kitchen and cooking – a glass of wine, good music, great smelling and tasting foods. When I was younger I was working a lot and in evenings my mother's food seldom was enough, so I learned to make pancakes, shepherd's pie and goulash soup... I was about 11-12yrs old as I remember it was the time of U2's earliest albums that I knew all the words to, even as a child. Anyway when I left school and went to college in Waterford Ireland, the landlady fed us 4 days a week and since I was working weekends I would eat at home, either at mothers or with friends over weekends. It was a good setup but the food wasn't great. In 1989 I got my own place for real and bought a cook book, I learned a lot then too, but still basics. When I got married and had first kids it was often the common Swedish food basics that were made but sometimes I would dare to be experimental and do woks and spicy stuff. After working in New Orleans in 1998 I met Cajun food for the first time and was sold directly, fantastic food and culture. In the last few years I have also experimented and made up some good dishes as I go along, so I look forward to having you around for dinners and good wine and some good music… maybe even dance around in the kitchen, who knows… I love to dance, even if ungracefully.

Soon the people will be getting ready to put out the breakfast here at the backpackers' hotel– it's horrible, no-one eats it and most go to union café 5 minutes away as they have some great food there. I don't feel hungry at all and we will stop at 9am, after 1,5hrs on bus for water etc. so I may just skip it. Dinner last night was delayed and it took 1,5hrs for delivery. The group like when I am asking for them to the waiters, so I try to come up with some diplomatic ways to ask the waiters etc. – last night I asked if we had to wait for the entire chicken's lifetime before it would be mature enough to eat… he didn't get it… just smiled and said Hakuna Matata.

On the way home a street trader asked if I was interested in Bob Marley – of course – cool so you want some herbal spices – weed. No, not tonight my dear brother from a different mother… he had anything I wanted and could get more in 5 minutes – forget it… happy that it's easy to say no. We can see young people here stoned daily, eyes dead and bodies sick… We were advised not to take taxis with motorbikes as the drivers are often stoned or drunk… still though I haven't seen or heard of any accidents while here – but I cannot read the papers. Yesterday some kids made a fire with car tires – so there was black smoke all over our area of the city, really not the nicest scent, it reminded me of Belfast at the end of the 1980's.

It is strange how quickly the rhythm changes from Sweden's speed and long days to Africa's slowness and darkness in early evenings – that alone is a culture shock – not having light enough, but then again we are out from 0800-1700 daily so we get have of course plenty of fresh air…

Next week's project will focus on getting the pathway and shelter finished, we will have the kids only on Tuesday to Thursday and then they will leave. Then there will just be a week left with a team of 6-7 people for the last of my weeks here. The chairs we got (80 pieces) will come on Monday, and the material for the tables too, I really hope we will see all the completed units before going home, that would be a great success. The tables will be from metal frames and wooden tops... if all goes to plan we will make them at the school too, that would be a nice way to end here.

I read again parts of your most recent email, about your wedding and the months afterwards – it must have been a tough time and also as you say keeping a face outwards that no-one was to know. I think we went through similar times but with different issues, some sad and tough times when not agreeing on teamwork at home and sharing and our world travels.

In my case, I could have adjusted the travels and schedules but they were still needed in order to manage the 4 kids growing needs as well as a more and expensive household and wifestyle (new word). Some specific times I remember just feeling like the provider of money and that's all, there was no relation or closeness or great family times after about 2005/2006 – it just wasn't there. Now I know myself better too and know that I have a lot to give and learn and share and see with people close to me, people that I know in a pure way through dialog and respect and listening more than talking (note to self: need to get better at that still) – talk far too much at times...

Wi-Fi has limited access just now... ☹ - hope it gets up and running soon so I can send before leaving in an hour...

Woke to a smile in your eyes

Felt your presence in the wildest of adventures

A calm awareness of trust and discovery

I like to feel you close

Woke from a dream that once had died

Felt you near as we find new paths

A new truth as stories collide

Simple elegant differences and all so wondrous

Woke knowing that it's a day closer

To see you and smile and laugh and share

Felt warm, close and just waiting

To see beauty as you open your eyes

I hope you have a wonderful start of your holiday, I look forward to hear of your adventures too, you know… I am sure you have had and will have lots, how I look forward to sharing some of them.

At 730am we left the backpackers hotel with Comfort (name of the driver) in a 9 seater jeep heading for Tarangire national park. It was to take 4hrs, so I guessed 8hrs but it worked out ok. We stopped first for water (and my breakfast) at 9am since I didn't make union café at 7am as I wanted… and the reason was change of project.

We had hoped a new project would be approved for the last week of our 4 with Godfrey, so that we could rebuild a kitchen at the school, as it's a horrible place. We got word today at 655am that the project would be done soon but unfortunately not by us...hhhmmmm.... So the issue was what we would do in the last week as we finish our intended project a week earlier than expected. Now its solved – in the last week we will work at a Maasai village and build the teachers house so they can stay and not have to skip work because of rain... all good. What was great was that all volunteers here said they would join, no question, wherever we are needed. The team is quite close now so it was cool that all agreed independently. I felt sad that I would just Godfrey for a few more days.

We stopped at a gas station in middle of nowhere and it was a real westernized gas station, toilets, supermarket etc... – I got a Snickers and some coke and off we went. The next city was Arusha and this city is famous as it hosts the courthouse where the Rwanda trials for genocide were held. We saw the actual courthouse as we passed through, scary to think what was discussed and shown as evidence in there. We got to the park at 1130am (kept good time, unusual for Africa), first we ate lunch and then in we went, within a few minutes we saw the zebras and impalas – just hanging out in the sun... really cool. Then on to the elephants – it was really warm and we caught them on the way to the lake that Comfort knew about, so we went there and watched them arrive and drink – very cool.

After that it was gnu, baboon, more elephants, warthogs, more elephants, giraffes of all sorts, near the end we even saw a cheetah eating an impala for lunch – nice. The safari day ended with a 150km drive to a Lutheran hostel and that is where we stay 2 nights – dinner at a bar across the street was also fantastic along with a couple of Kilimanjaro beers.

Today I listened to a lot of old U2 music, the innocence of coming of age. I wondered what you were doing, how you were feeling, what plans you have in your head, you are so booked up this autumn that I really hope we can both prioritize well and balanced, I know work comes first a lot but at the same time I want to see you a lot and often and share all we can share – so happy to be there soon. I am so tired and tomorrow we all get up at 630am as we have Ngorongoro drive tomorrow.

630am Sunday morning – been awake a while in a black dark room in Africa, it's a nice comfort - all part of the Safari package, good shower, fast food (within 20 minutes) and the gang all feel happy about today's adventures. We leave at 8am and should get to the Ngorongoro park by 930am. We come back here tonight also.

I lay here thinking, my mind drifts towards the spiritual aspects of life. Around the campfire last night we spoke of the American religions, and also of Christian, Muslim and Hindu and how there are all about having a set of beliefs and rules and things to hold on to. I feel so far from that now. I feel here in the pure air of an African spirit, that it may be as simple as leading a good, honest, simple life and spending time with people who energize and create and who have strong value awareness, who also try to be simple and honest. I feel very much we need time to discover these great things about each other. You are very well along this path and my move to Kristianstad will create free time from driving and will help with being more at peace with myself, and brings me closer to you, the airport, my work, my colleagues, I feel very happy about all that. This will be a great next few months and I am so very happy. Now it's time to get up. I wish you a wonderful Sunday. I expect you will see these notes on Monday evening as we go to Moshi before leaving for Maasai village for last week, starting there on Tuesday morning. Many hugs from this distant place, wishing I was closer to you.

4pm Sunday evening – got your sms just now as I arrive back at hostel, no Wi-Fi...damn it - but still time to write now as dinner is not for a while yet. Today was big-five-day at safari – we saw three of them, the lion, elephant and buffalo, the rhino and the leopard were avoiding us. We did see a cheetah yesterday though. It's amazing to see them all in their natural places and doing as they normally do... eating and killing and drinking etc. – we saw one lion close to a pack of hyenas and our guide said that most likely the lion killed the animal (whatever it was) and then the hyenas chased off the lion... bummer. Saw a hippo and some warthogs, gazelles and gnus – loads and loads, a very nice day and no speed just calmly driving through. There were many people there too and lots of safari jeeps – hundreds actually, but the area we were in was 260square km so all was free and easy. I would really like if you had been there, I saw from one of your Facebook pix that you were close to a leopard, where was that photo taken? Looked cool, do you like to see animals? I do, but not in zoos if possible...

On the way back from the park I was wondering what you were doing today and what your normal free time looks like. I am often in the mood to do stuff at home with good music on and fixing stuff, when I get bored I make new projects like moving sofa and try to reorganize bedroom for example. When I arrive in Kristianstad I will have blank walls. I don't like to fill them fast as I like to wait a while.

I will have my own washing machine too in my apartment – first time for that. Do you have a dryer? A dishwasher? I don't have any and may skip both but will see how all starts off once there. If I remember rightly your home office is your kitchen table, mine was too in Karlskrona but have a room now in Kristianstad instead, as well as a spare room to rent/loan out if needed, haven't really decided yet how what to do there... even though starting alone might be best as we talked/mailed about before.

Some historical stuff now for a change, if ok for you...

Father was one of 14 kids and 5 of those died very young, he was born in 1916 - a very famous year in Irish history. That year when father was just a couple of months old the beginning of the Republic of Ireland came about. There was another mini war against the British that became famous mainly because they killed the main seven guys behind it. If they had rotted in jail maybe nothing would have happened but they were executed instead. There was outrage and a guy called Michael Collins became famous for first bringing the British to their knees and then by signing a treaty which led to the creation of Northern Ireland... some very long stories about this time... we will be busy talking you know.

I wasn't exposed much to the war in Northern Ireland but did travel there a lot at the end of the 1980's, when it was most dangerous actually but we didn't know that at the time. As usual we knew that the TV was very biased (BBC) so the news reported wasn't always an account of the day to day actual events. Living in Belfast was always frightening, being constantly monitored by helicopters and where I lived in the Catholic area, we were always under surveillance. There was daily intimidation and police checks and everyday there was someone pointed a gun at me. I remember going to a graduation ball there once at the Europa hotel and at the very beginning the host/arranger of the evening welcomed us to the 'most bombed hotel in Europe – enjoy the evening'. At the end of the evening we took a taxi home, there was a separate line for taxis, one for Catholics and one for Protestants... felt a bit like Martin Luther King's stories of 'whites only'.... I remember also meeting a girl there who had the most waxed/gel filler hair I had ever seen, when you touched it, it was rock hard. Seems strange the funny elements that just pop into memory.

In 2016 at Easter maybe we can go to Dublin to see some interesting anniversary events I am sure. Ireland has had a tourist concept called 'the gathering' going on for a few years now – I think it was intended to bring people home... a friend of mine told me recently that there are over 90 million Irish passports in the world, I don't how true it is but it means there are over 7 billion wannabees....

Back to father now - by the time he was 15 he had lost 5 of his siblings through various diseases, cannot remember which, now when I think of it. I never met his parents and on mother's side of the family I only knew my grandfather until I was 6, he died in 1977, my grandmother (mothers mother) died when I was 1 so I have no memory of her, even if there a number of photos. Two of father's sisters were nuns and teachers in Malaysia, only one of them wanted to be a teacher and the other was forced to be one, they were sent away to Malaysia by the convent, I think this was in the 1950's. At the same time my mother's aunt was also a nun in Rhodesia (now called something else – not sure but could be Zimbabwe or Mozambique...) and mother also had an aunt in Ireland who worked in a Magdalena Sister's convent – a place where fallen girls had to go (girls who were pregnant or 'knocked up' – Irish slang for being pregnant). If you see the movie 'Philomena' you will recognize the story. My mum also had a cousin who was a priest and we also knew he loved being away on different missions in Africa. A few years ago I was in Dublin and bought a book called 'All the bishops men' – a book about child sex abuse in the church, there was a whole chapter about my cousin. I never knew, and there were photos within our family of him at my house, you will see sometime if you visit Ireland with me, Kate has them. No-one in my family knew about this at all... scary that just by random chance I found out...

Anyway again back to father, he inherited his father's farm after his father and brother died – and there is a photo of him looking very handsome in his 30's again that Kate has... we will just have to go see Kate too. He had no tractor and just 7 cows when he married mother in 1963. When I was born he had 10 cows and at most we had 14, we never had a bull. Whenever we had calves it was my job from 4years old to take care of them, feeding them and cleaning them for market etc... any time a cow would be calving I would stay up with father and help him if needed. I overcame my childhood fear of darkness because of such a situation.

One night/early morning, one of our cows was having her calf and our cows were always chained to the wall, the chain hanging loosely around their necks. This cow had some problems with the calf and it was very hard to help her but we eventually got the calf out, but it looked dead, tongue hanging out and white eyes, father was upset. I was just angry, so I kicked the calf in the stomach and it coughed and came around – alive – father was so happy and he hugged me and the calf. But then we noticed the cow wasn't moving at all, when we went to let her chain off she was choking, dying slowly... father told me to get a hacksaw from the car... 200m away in the dark with no light, I was so afraid, he just told me to go and forget the dark, just get on with it. I ran as fast as I could, seeing ghosts in my imagination but kept running, when I got to the car where the tool was I just opened it and the hacksaw just fell out, now to run back... same ghosts and scary faces but I kept running, I got to the cow and cut her chain and she fell over, so I did the same again, kicked her and father was again upset and crying, it's no use, she's gone he said, 'no' I screamed and kicked her again and again and she coughed and found breath, it was the best moment of my life at that time, father helped the cow to the calf and all was saved, I was the hero at home for weeks, and I got to keep the calf, his name was Toby. That cow often would cry when I fed her and I would hug her a lot when she did, I was close to cows a lot as a child... there are many cow stories too, and I love to talk about those farm times – 'picking up the pennies' also, another interesting story.

'Lucky to be born poor' was the name of a book I was to write a number of years ago and I believe this is still true. Mother was a great entrepreneur, she was great at knitting and baking and most people knew this. When I was very young she would knit by hand and make those beautiful Irish Aran sweaters (will get you one in Ireland – you see – we will just have to go....). As mother became locally well known for this, people asked her to make school sweaters also for the school uniforms. So she invested in a machine when I was about 5-6years old. Every day she could manage to make 2-3 sweaters and often earned more from this than father did from cows, he was annoyed by this at times, but still we had some money and it was all needed of course...

My first taste of being an entrepreneur was when I was maybe 7-8 years old. Father would often have planted far too many vegetables and we would end up dumping them or giving to the cows as there were just too many. So one Saturday I was back from hunting and father was fixing the cows, I collected a bag of vegetables and went the neighbor's houses and asked if they would want to buy some. 'Does your father know?' – NO… 'ok, then give me a good price…' and so it began, I started selling fathers vegetables to neighbors and making deals about carrots, onions, potatoes, Brussel sprouts etc…, and made some money, in the first two months I made nearly as much as father. I told him that the calves were eating more so I needed the vegetables, he never questioned this as that was my job. Once I had to run to local shop to buy back my own turnips so they wouldn't be noticed as missing… messy.

After about 2 months by chance mother had made a deal with the same shop to sell cakes there, she had her small money box with Dempsey on it and her earnings were there… I had a similar one and one day they got mixed, in mine was about £25 and in hers should have been about £12… the owners daughter mixed this up when mother was collecting and so I was caught… I came home from school and mother had some questions and I was badly beaten up for lying…. Father never stepped in and this was the saddest part and that remained with me a long time… a few days' later neighbors started to call to the house to buy more and more and mother realized her mistake… I never forgave her. Then father started sowing more and selling for real and we became great partners, I was 9 at most.

'Cabbage plants for sale' – we had our own cabbage as I wrote before, they come from small seeds. We had an old fashioned machine that wasted a lot of seeds. When these seeds grew they were too close to each other so father would 'thin them out' and basically throw 80% of them away. This seemed to be the correct procedure as far as I know at least. One day when I was by chance looking at the local paper I saw a small advert, cabbage plants needed… I asked father – nope, nothing he could do… so I asked if I could use some of the unused vegetable land, 'for what?' just yes or no, 'ok, go on then'. So each time father took away 4 from 5 plants I took them and learned how to sow them again. Our neighbor was the editor of the local paper and I asked if I could put an advert in his paper for cabbage plants – of course – for £5. I had that but I needed to make a sign using paint so I told him I would pay £3, he said no until I told him my entire plan... then he said yes. So in a week – there was a newspaper advert and a sign at our gate to sell cabbage plants – we made a fortune, those months I earned more than father... this time there was no beating but he did feel embarrassed... I was not yet 10.

The year I became 10 I got my first real job getting paid by the hour. I had picked strawberries for 6 years at a local farm and was quite sick of slow pace and same poor strawberries. In 1980 we all heard of a very tough aggressive farmer called Jim Kehoe. Everyone was afraid of him as he was a senior boxer and tough hard man. He became like a second father to me between ages 10-19. I loved that man.

He was the oldest of 4 brothers and the most experienced in our county regarding strawberries as well as other fruits and vegetables but in 1980 all I knew was that he knew strawberries. Anyway I decided to go to his farm instead of our local one. At that farm the strawberries were huge and plentiful, I fitted in directly and immediately earned twice as much as my family members while they worked on other farms where the managers were nicer, Jim was tough but fair. In 1981 I worked there again and at the end of the season Jim asked me if I wanted to work after the season doing other work on his huge farm, I was so happy, I said yes directly and when I was 10 I officially earned more per day than father. I was proud of me for the first time, even though I got none of this money myself I was happy to contribute at home and to my sister's college education. I never really thanked Jim for this time but working with him gave picking up pennies a new meaning, if you worked hard in one job, others will come... I was proof of that.

This obviously is a very detailed and long text about my past I hope you have managed to get through it ok. I sat at dinner this evening and thought of you being at home and fixing stuff then enjoying evening sun... you wrote that you turned lobster, did you know that Irish and Scottish people have sun issues? Yes, it's true. We are originally blue and after three weeks in sun we go white for a few minutes then its lobster alert, we are not good with sun at all. It is funny after writing so much I am sure I am repeating some stuff, most likely far too much.

Hope you got to read at the beach like you wrote, look forward very much to see your mails tomorrow evening, happy to go home slowly tomorrow and see some village life, plan to buy some nice paintings also if possible... nice with some new stuff for new place... anyway goodnight take care and see you now even sooner. Many hugs – precious you XX

645am Monday

I realize that I didn't really describe the safari so well just that I saw lots of stuff. When there I thought a lot of the expanse of space and how these 25000+ animals all lived in this ecosystem and were able to manage to survive and exist over years of both evolution and huge world changes. There are but animals but still live in flocks, herds, packs, prides, all with their own social habits and ways of working together, how they hunt, take care of each other, scavenge for food... all this was happening right in front of our eyes, each day just another to survive, eating, resting and protecting each other. I often think we can learn a lot from animals, they often have a very simple life and just hang out, it's only our brains have made us the top of the food chain. Animals have an enormous respect for each other and its comes naturally for them but at the same time its survival of the fittest that counts daily as being chased by lions or hyenas or jackals cannot be an easy task, it sure keeps them fit though.

Today will be a slow drive home, we leave at 830 to see a local village and how its day to day life looks like, I hope to buy some art there, Maasai pictures for my new place. Later we will go to the Africa culture center in Arusha for a walk and guided tour there, we are to get home at 430-500 but since its Africana time – we never really know...

Lunch is to be a local beef bar b q at the village we visit. Tonight it's back to Moshi and the backpacker's hotel, then to the new village early tomorrow for last 4 days of work, cement and sand and plastering is on the agenda, a lot of cement to be carried.

Hope you are smiling that beautiful smile, many hugs – home soon to see you.... Take care of special you. XX

Monday evening 545pm

Back in Moshi all meeting and updating each other about weekend, seems like everyone really enjoyed their different activities, some went hiking, others went to a lake to kayak (damn I missed that – next weekend – maybe). We tell of the safari. I split now from group to find Wi-Fi and its limited access.... more to write before I send.

The craft shop run by local carpenters – most amazing. No matter what price they asked for they enjoyed bargaining and making deals. You could decorate a complete house for what we say that day. If you wanted tables chairs whatever – they could make it. A really cool place.

Even though today was not safari we did do some shopping at a small town that we were passing before going on a great culture walk and got to see the normal life of the tribes all living together in one of the most multi tribal towns of the area.

I have seen some really beautiful paintings in different places and have had a hard time to decide – today was easy so I bought 2 paintings, one beautiful and colorful and one black and white, I also bought some Maasai tartan material, will explain later... valued at 131$ and I paid 93$...bargain hunters, it would be cool to make a movie of these situations.

The kids ran their cows in front of cars so people would stop to give water, some cows died as a result. We stopped and gave what we had, the two boys fought over what we gave them.

We first saw the carpenters – the guys who carve all those heads and long legged Maasai warrior souvenirs – that was really cool to see and I bought an ebony wooden club there – value of 35$ and I paid 18$ - you will see. After that we were guided through about 5 different tribal houses where the daily life was explained to us by the guide, we saw the making of banana beer and wine (wine was like strong cider – nice). We then went to the Maasai painters and of course I just had to buy there, really nice stuff for 40$ and I paid 27$. I love bargaining where and when I can, and I think the locals also enjoy.

After all was bought we had a local bar b q — beef and vegetables and chips — so nice. Then we had a long drive and went to the culture center of Arusha. A place that Bill Clinton had been to in 2000… don't know why — but maybe he started hanging out with Bono after that.

We didn't stay too long there as it was far too commercial and all prices were fixed… no fun negotiating then.

Then it was a race to get to Moshi before 5pm as one of the gang needed to get money through western union bank, but police checks and roadblocks and traffic limited us so we didn't make it. She has nothing and needs 200$ to fly home on Friday — I will give it, if it all goes bananas for her… will get her father's western union codes so I can get the cash on Saturday if it comes to that, there is no western union in our village…

Tomorrow its back to work, cement and everything connected, feels good after 4 days off, and they went fast and very well — very happy, have lots of good photos and will upload when possible… off to bank now… hope to catch you later. Many many hugs — I miss chatting and having contact directly with you but do like writing as you maybe have understood well by now… see u soon…. XX

When the sun rises and brings the damn

I think of you

When the day's work is planned before us

I think of you

When the quiet moments in a busy day arrive

I think of you

When the evenings calm arrives after another hard day

I think of you

When the night ends another day of wonder

I think of you

I think of you

And the time seems to pass easily

I think of you

And the issues of daily life become less complex

I think of you

And the moments to share are so desired

I think of you

And the pains of the past seem relieved

I think of you

And the future seems brighter and warmer

I think of you

And I smile a big smile

I think of you

You may have noticed

Tuesday 720pm

I feel totally wrecked, so tired – today was toughest yet for me even though none of the team sweated enough together to need a shower – I am just back from there and could sleep now. Godfrey likes both how I lead and direct but also that I stay after if needed and that was the case today. We had left the hotel at 800am for the 1hr drive to get here – first we had to stop at bank then just before halfway to the village the project leader Rachel had forgotten the keys so we had to go back. Then just about 10 minutes before the village turnoff we stopped by a place to check out leaving dinner for the 5 kids for Thursday night. What a place – we are in the middle of the rainforest and we find a paradise lost... some photos taken, honestly it was a great place – a whisky bar no less... as we drive away all I could think of was The Doors – Alabama song – 'show me the way to the next whisky bar, oh don't ask why, oh don't ask why' Anyway we got to work at 1030am to meet Godfrey, he hugged me – happy to see me again, as I was to see him, feel close to him, I like that a lot – they had done so much work it was unbelievable and so well done, I couldn't wait to get started and organized.

So off we went, Rachel and I, to plan a new section that I had suggested to Godfrey last week – now it would be done and it meant that the kids could walk all the way to dining hall and not need to be away from a footpath and always under cover. I was so happy we have enough material and resources and determination to get a great job started and with good results expected.

We also handed over 2,625million Tanzanian shillings – about 1200€ to the school for the tables and school benches needed for the dining room, we had handed over 400€ last week to get material for desks. The school head teacher Bella blessed us and thought we had contributed over and above any previous group, I felt so happy.

In the afternoon we made additional unplanned progress again with our own initiatives and drive, well done to the team and excellent team spirit – this is a strong group and very willing to get stuck in. As we neared 4pm Godfrey showed me the last step of plastering that was needed and asked me to stay, of course. So all went home and I got to work, heavy hard and bad back position was killing me and by 530 I was about to go home but Godfrey in his sweet and soft voice (just like father) asked 'a short while more, soa soa (ok)?' you just cannot say no, so another 45 minutes then he hugged me and said 'friend' – I was proud, happy and destroyed. When I got home dinner was ready but half the gang had walked for 2hrs, they got home 2minutes after me, great – dinner is served.

After dinner all said no to showers as most took it easy all day. I had to shower as I covered in plaster from my lack of skill... and sweating from earlier activities during day. Now its writing time... don't know how long I will last – feel so tired. All play Uno as usual – feel fine to step out, will play a round later if still awake, it's Jim Morrison time – Riders on the storm... excellent ... fits my mood. Today you were to fly to Poland, hope it went well, and that meeting your grandmother too will be a nice and positive feeling. I was sad when I read about your father's stroke. I have often had one of my father's lines in my head. The day before he died, he was lucid enough to just recognize me and he said in his soft sweet voice 'live before you die' these were the last words he spoke to me on August 5th 1990. 24yrs later I move to a new place – taking my time to start this period of life – but cannot wait to do so, as it also means a new closeness in both mind and body to you and an autumn filled with new exciting challenges and adventures that I hope we can share a lot of.

When I think of my father he was already old, 55 when I was born, so we seldom played football or had any real strong modern father son relation but I loved him above all else and think of him every day.

When mother died I felt sad briefly more so for my brother as he both lived with her longest as well as he found her after she died... after about 1yr I felt a sense of relief though. I knew I would never have an adult within family to steer me or my time to make demands or ask too much of me... sounds strange as I miss father still but it's how I felt. He had had two heart attacks and died of massive stroke on August 7th 1990. He had been sick since early in that year and in June he had his first heart attack, I had felt all year he would die. I listened daily to a song called 'If you go' by Hothouse Flowers, I have cried a thousand times to that song, check it out on Spotify... it is a classic, that turns me inside out every time... if I want to dream of my father I listen to this... will do that now too... just a moment – ah yes –

If you go

I hope you get there

If you get there

I hope you like it

If you go

.....

Anyway after the earlier stories of negotiation before and when I was 10 it all calmed down a while until I was 13½. On November 8th 1984, at about 630pm father broke his leg, it was one of two most significant moments leading me to be me. Sorry to go back and forth in time about him.

Earlier that year, father was asked by the government along with other farmers to expand and make more milk for export… father was reluctant but he dreamed of me taking over so he asked if I would study farming to continue and develop his farm – of course. I spent every available hour farming, either with father or Jim Kehoe (will describe him later). So father invested, he borrowed money from his sister and he bought more cows and a milk tank. I was so happy and he was so full of life and desire for this, I was his right hand, all said so and I felt so. I was physically very strong also at this time and I know I could do any of the jobs on the farm.

A couple of years before he had crushed a finger in a tractor accident and needed to get it partially removed. During that time mother hired a guy to fix the cows and farm, I was so pissed, I wanted to do it but school demanded I was to be there… my other boss Jim needed me too so I couldn't do it. Shite. When father broke his leg in 1984 it was the end of all those expansion dreams, in the space of 2 months all his and my dreams were dead in every way. He broke his leg on a Thursday evening. After the ambulance took him at 8pm mother asked me to finish off milking the cows and then she would ask the same guy to come work for a week as father would only need a week according to the ambulance first diagnosis. NO WAY, I wouldn't let that guy near our precious cows again – I didn't ask – I told mother I would study at home and take care of the farm, no-one believed I could, except father. The day after at the hospital mother asked father in front of me if I could manage it and he said 'I would trust no-one else to' I was so happy he said so. On the following Monday mother went to my school and told the story and that was that, I would stay at home and do what was needed until father was up and about... a real chance to prove myself, Jim gave me time off but asked me to work a few hours on Saturdays and Sundays – of course.

About a week after father went to hospital we expected him home but he had had some issues so he was moved to another hospital and would stay there for 2 more weeks and he would need rehab a longer time... we were all devastated. Father and I more than all the others. He told me in early December that he wouldn't come back to the farm ever again and that I was to organize the slaughter of all our cows except one. I was never so low in my life... devastated I asked him to reconsider, we could still make it, it was possible, anything was possible, I knew, but he wouldn't believe enough. I fought with him when he came home in December but to no avail.

Just before New Year's Eve in 1984, one Thursday morning my cousin Sean came with his big cattle trailer to load 13 cows into it, to go to Clohamon meat factory. Father wouldn't talk to me that day, except for one line – 'help them pass calmly'– I cried inside but held a straight face... (I am crying as I write this now) and off we went. Cousin Sean was about 40 at the time and a big farmer and had tools and machines etc... and was a great mechanic but a poor carpenter. About halfway to the factory the floor broke in the trailer and one cow had her leg against the road, a passer-by in a car told us. We stopped and had to let the cows out and from under the trailer I pushed the cows leg up, I cut myself badly on both my legs from the road and my arms from the broken trailer pieces, Sean saw this 'I don't have time to bleed' I said. It became a famous movie line, that I even used here in Africa. The cows we let out started to wander off up the road so I had to chase them, blood pouring and all... quite messy.

We got to the factory walking the cows. When we had checked them in for the executioner, I tried to calm them by massaging their frightened faces, something I had learned to do when we would have taken their calves to market. They would be sad for a few days afterwards and each day I would take care of them. My heart was pounding when the executions took place and as I watched them all fall, killed by the humane killer gun, I was shaking each time.

In some telepathic way I felt father knew when each shot killed each cow, I cried each time as they fell lifeless in front of me, (crying again now), it is still a strong intense memory after 30yrs.

We got back home after I collected the money at about 3pm. Father was so cold to me when I got home, he didn't say a word, just slapped me as hard as he could across my face and then hugged me (the only time ever) and I cried so much all evening with him, no-one spoke. The next day he said for the first time (of two) that he was proud of me. Father never told me that he loved me.

The dream was over – one cow left, I went back to school early in January – all the teachers knew what I had done and what I had been through – they welcomed me back and I felt good but so empty. Jim came by and offered me a job to work mornings and evenings if I wanted so I could learn more on my journey to college to study agriculture. Father was sad as he wanted me to be home with him but I went with Jim, we needed the money, it was a twisted time in my life.

An episode that also happening during this time when father was in hospital, was when the gypsies had let their donkeys graze our land and were intentionally and systematically doing this. So one Saturday evening my brother and I took 8 of them into one of our sheds for 'safe-keeping'. On Sunday at about 11am the local gypsy king arrived and asked for them.

I told them they were locked up and it would cost £200 to get them out, 'what? Your father usually takes a fiver (£5) and lets us take them away', so I looked around and then said 'he isn't here, you deal with me – and I will shoot one horse per hour until you pay' – 'no you fucking won't' he screamed, so I aimed the shotgun in his face – 'don't tempt me' he was so afraid and ran off. About an hour later he came back with 2 heavies, mother was afraid, 'they fall harder' I said and took the gun and three bullets. 'see you later' I told her and my brother came along, very reluctantly, 'what are you gonna do?' he said – 'I am going to shoot a horse'. The gypsy king had £100 and demanded his horses. I said no. I had my brother open the door of the locked shed – I went in, and in about 30 seconds – a gunshot. I came out. 'Now you have one horse less', I kept the gun pointed at the king – 'you need to get £200 for your 7 cows'... 'Fuck you' – I turned to go back in – 'stop, for Christ sake' – 'what?' 'here is your £200 now let me have my horses' and he threw it on the ground, 'pick it up and hand it to me' so he did and the 2 heavies couldn't believe a 13yr old telling the king this – they couldn't do anything – he handed me £200 and my brother let out all the horses, all 8. I had shot through the window. The gypsy king placed some curse in their local language and took them, one of the heavies thanked me for not shooting any horse, I just told him I would next time and would not hesitate.

Father wasn't happy about that episode, mother got the money and gave me £50 - 'you have some balls'... I was very happy and knew I had something inside that could be of benefit. Father had always tried to please the gypsies in different small ways – I refused to. There are few other hay stealing stories too. One in particular also included a shooting. Father had many bullets or cartridges to be more precise – it was possible to take out the lead shot and replace with corn seeds. So we had about 20 of these cartridges. Our hay was constantly being robbed and we suspected the gypsies. One night while we were on watch, very late at night, a guy came and started to pull bales, father had never shot at anyone and hesitated, he wouldn't – I took the gun and shoot the guy in the legs, he couldn't get up, his legs burning... I hit him in the face with the butt of the gun... he sat there very confused and dazed. With a gun in his face he admitted it was him all the time. He wasn't bleeding but so sore, father knew him and his father so we traded 100hrs of farm work with father and me for what he had stolen. The cops would never know. Good thing too as father was still responsible and I shouldn't be using his gun at 14... even as a farmer's son his license didn't cover that...

Ok time for bed, 2400 words tonight – good.

I hope all is fine with precious you, soon I am home to share those saved hugs, thought of you a lot today from both a personal and professional perspective, we can do a lot together and that may benefit us both at work and in private. I like this, we have so much to discover. I plan a weekend in Ireland at some point as well as Milan possibly before Christmas, will see how works develops, have Australia trip too... so much, as well as move and redesign new place – so happy for all activities. Many hugs – as well as all saved ones – look forward to all we plan and will discover – goodnight XX.

Wednesday 515pm

Just got your sms from 0840 this morning, seems like you had a long drive on bumpy roads – I have never seen worse roads than those here, totally bonkers trying to drive and then on main roads there are few rules, if any. It seems more like a few poor loosely written guidelines – that's it, just like in China The condition of the cars also are terrible, a very low % would pass the MOT car tests back home.

So after 2-3 weeks you write in your mails that you get itchy feet and need new projects – we are too alike – I love planning and executing projects, hiking, travelling, discovering and enjoying fresh free air – it's a great feeling... a lot to do together I hope during coming times ☺.

Today went very fast. Last week I had suggested if we would have enough material that we make a new pathway so that the kids would not walk through rainwater to get to the dining hall (where, by the way, your chairs arrived for today). No-one thought we could do it in time but yesterday I took the team there and said that we need to split the group and delegate work well in the gang, so we would finish on Friday, most were skeptical. This evening we go home with maybe half a day really left, will definitely be finished our work by tomorrow evening, all are so happy and satisfied – feels great to have led them through this together with the project team and the fundi (builder). Even this evening I worked later than everyone else – it's been a habit for years – get it done, then go home. Most went for a long walk now, normally I would to but I wanted to write just now instead, and soon to have a shower, covered in cement just now... and smelly, sweated a lot today to get work finished with the gang... ☺

The 5 kids leave tomorrow night, they feel very emotional, and would like to follow us on our last week, but that's how it goes. All are going home to at least a month of holidays, I am sure they will never forget this time. They start to pack and realize it's just this last night with us and then a few hours tomorrow and then they leave. What they don't know is that tomorrow we finish early to have tea at Godfreys house, then we go to dinner at the place called 'the whisky bar'... really cool place, will have photos for sure as words couldn't describe it.

Then we will be 9 left, 5 go off to sun and sandy beaches for weekend, I stay in Moshi and will do some trips with those who are left – kayak to Kenya sounds really cool, especially since I cannot swim ... oh well. I will need to learn some time, the lake we kayak across is 3500m deep, a sunken volcano. We move to the Maasai village on Tuesday so after tomorrow and an easy Friday morning we will have just 4 days left... feels like I have been here a long time, the routine is so engrained already, so I'm happy to go to another village to see what that life is like.

When awake last night I let myself drift into thoughts of seeing you after all these stories, see you live in front of me, hearing your voice and listening to you laughing. I miss that even though we met so briefly and usually with me having to run off, will be nice to not have to run away.

Since you too have travelled and lived in many places – then which are your favorite cities? I like Bangkok, Paris, Dublin, Hamburg,

Chicago and all for very different reasons, but all having one thing in common I have spent a lot of time there and really enjoyed the people and culture of those cities.

During my time in IKEA I was in Bangkok many times and really liked it a lot, partied a lot as well as worked hard with both trainings and running Kaizen events (week-long improvement projects), we had our best ever results in Bangkok and also a large nail in my IKEA coffin happened there.

I was given the opportunity to have 100+ Asian suppliers at a COPQ seminar (COPQ means cost of poor quality – it was the subject of my first book). I relished the idea of this seminar, some high up people were there too and of course I had to use that opportunity to impress them... I did so in a very negative way. We had spent many months working on the COPQ concept and they all knew our ideas well and ambitions through the guys at headquarters. So my usual starting point – a slide from Jim Collins brilliant book 'Good to Great' – Hedgehog Concept... you know it for sure. Anyway after that slide it's about the theory of constraints writer Goldwraith and his book The Goal. This book is about a company manager, Alex, and his need for realizing the true meaning of his and others role as he searches for this meaning with the help of Jonah. Jonah has an answer that proves shocking to all but so simple and clear that it's amazing that this book is not the only bible needed to run a business.

In the middle of this book there is a moment when Jonah reveals the secret of all businesses – to make money... how simple could it be. So here I am in the middle of a presentation and I ask the question to the audience of 1000+ what is the goal of your company? No-one answers so I take the chance ask our own high up guys, come on, come on up here and tell us – what is the goal of

IKEA, so one comes up all proud and tall, the goal of IKEA is growth, thanks, you are wrong, anyone else? 'what', 'yes you are wrong the goal of IKEA is not growth, thanks, now sit down', he was not a 'happy camper' as we say in Ireland.

So I ask again – what is the goal of your company? And at the far end of the audience a small guy puts up his hand and whispers 'make money' What? Make money – perfect, I ran through the crowd, stood him up and said – the only honest man in the house... I was given the black eyes for the rest of the day from my own team... I didn't care – COPQ was already a European success story and this was capturing Asia, it went down a storm, I was so happy but knew I was definitely on the company's 'bad guy' radar now but the story is still told (or written), most like it though...

It's now 9pm, dinner gone, a glass of wine, a beer, sounds like a cool evening, it's actually quiet, a few have gone to bed the last remaining few discuss the weekend bookings. Just now a discussion about Max and McDonalds in Sweden. It's mad here you know. And then there was a discussion about being a beard police man...a police man who checks that beards are grown properly... I didn't get it at all.

Do you know Malika Ayanye? An Italian singer, absolutely brilliant, bubbly bar music, it's on my iPod just now... nice.

So to music. I grew up with U2 and have seen them more than 10 times, and have been following them since before they were called U2. At the same time one of favorite albums is 'The Wall' from Pink Floyd and it describes the process of growing up and the problems a boy has as he grows to man through relationships, marriage, being a rock n roll star and losing his mind in the end to eventually have a total collapse and 'the wall' falls. It's so fantastic, I saw the concert first in 1990 in Berlin and then again in 2012 in Stockholm and the last year again in Gothenburg. It's a great show. What shows have you seen? Concerts? Theatre? Opera? I am so curious, so much to learn about you and also to experience with you.

Thursday 9am

What was to be the last day of building turns into a washout, so much rain that we will not be mixing cement for a long time, damn it. We all got up and were ready but since I was awake between 0130-0330am I knew it was raining all night, we are in the rain forest after all and today it shows. If the rain follows usual pattern it will stop soon and we can work after 11, if not, we could be messed up for the day. There is paint work to be done and there are a few on that just now, but we are more the heavies and builders, we are the ones who got us the time to start to paint. So maybe we deserve a day with less activity, anyway I need to pack for weekend and next week, we leave this house in 24hrs for the last time.

Friday 645am

Just when I was settling into a couple of hours of writing yesterday along comes the builder, let's go, there was no way I thought we would start, but we did and it was miserable for a couple of hours, slipping and sliding, dropping wet things, tools hurting, but when we all pulled together and shared the misery we soon got going. By lunch the rain was gone, the wet clothes off and we were on target to finish, with just the detailed work that I did with Godfrey and Mesere, it was all ready by 3pm, everyone was so happy. The last plastering took about an hour and was heavy on my back but we were all so happy to be finished at last. At 430pm we went to

Godfreys home for pancakes and meat sauce, it was the first meat we ate all week, really good. His house is made of concrete unlike many others and we all sat in their sitting room. The house has 2 rooms, the other being a bedroom where he sleeps with wife and 3 kids – he has a bed, his kids don't. The kitchen is a separate building and there was no door from his bedroom, just out to the open. From his door opening to the cattle shed where he had 2 heifers (young female cows) was about 4 meters' maximum and to the chickens was about 2 meters, they were noisy all night he says but he couldn't afford a door just now.

I was both sad and angry and wanted to give so much to him, so he has my shoes as he asked for them, had he asked for more he would have got that too, he is the closest person to my father I have met for 20yrs, strange that he is younger than me...Louisa asked him if his daughter Jacqueline would go to secondary school next year, he didn't really answer, I was immediately thinking too much... come back to this later...

At 530pm we went to Kiliya village to get the bus, we stood and waited for the first time ever, strange feeling.... Anyway while there, a guy asked us guys how many cows we would sell the girls for.... No sale...

Friday 7pm

Back in Moshi - a roller coaster day – but will start with last night. We got bus to Kilawa lodge, a paradise in the woods, owned by a German who has lived there for the past 2 years with his wife, his kids still lived in Germany. It is called the 'The Whisky Bar', I think I mentioned before. We arrive at same time as kids (they had taxi as

During the last week at the rainforest village Godfrey asked me for my shoes... they were battered, broken and full of holes.... I am sure he fixed them up after

they are leaving soon) and then we find out that the youngest Chris was very homesick, couldn't wait to see his mother and he would see her today, (actually just about now he should be there) good for him. We sat out on the veranda with a view over the rainforest – so beautiful, we sat there an hour, had a beer, laughed and joked with the leaving kids. Then it was meal time by IKEA solar light since there was a power cut. Cozy. Nice food and good laughs. After the meal we had a short whisky tasting session, 4 different types and I was in charge of choice, I like good whisky (even if expensive). When all this was over, off we went on a bus for last night at the village. Slept well until rain woke me at about 2am, needed to pee after beer too, damn it, so out to the long-drop and with no power it was so very dark... anyway after some more sleep the mosque woke me at 4am... couldn't sleep again, again thinking of you and your days, nights, thoughts, favorite colors, songs, films, so much stuff.

I also began thinking of work again, going back to the world of Lean and 6Sigma but now with a broader view of what some things mean in a different world. A few Swedish kronor saved here and there, one life changes as we discuss sacking and firing and hiring and all the things that go along with it in Sweden, whereas here Godfrey has work for a few more weeks and after that he or I don't know… ☹, feel very sad about that…

I thought of buying companies and working with big projects about using some pictures from here in some presentations, feel very great about what has been done here – the real projects may start once I get home, a lot to talk about here…

I got up at 6 as we all had to get organized to leave the house, village, school, friends, it would be a long day. While packing I realized I had lost 2 small Maasai paintings I had bought, and they were similar but different colors… gone, I doubt anyone took them, so I guess I left them on the bus last Monday after the safari… shite. Anyway we got to work at 830 and Godfrey wasn't there yet, we just took lots and lots of photos – the chairs and tables had arrived ☺ ☺ - Bella, the school director, was so happy, it was really a cool moment – thank you for giving us that opportunity, you and a few others made it happen, thank you so much… you will see photos…

Once Godfrey arrived, we got going on the finishing touches for the project, he added a few things and also in parallel Louisa had, with our contributions, ordered skylights for all the rooms. It made such a difference and all were in place by this morning, we could see in the classrooms and staff room – fantastic.

The tables and chairs in place – just in time for last day. The kids were so excited and so were we. Thanks for your contribution, it was so welcome. They were made by a local guy so even the production was giving/contributing to locals – felt like a very important initiative for them and for us.

At tea time I had a chat with Louisa about the costs for a child to go to secondary school, she said about €700 for 4 years so most kids don't go. I asked her if she thought Godfrey would send his daughter, she didn't seem convinced by his lack of an answer. She said that she wasn't sure about costs but that Bella would know…. In my head all I could think was – he who saves one life, saves the world entire. Don't know why.

On the last day we also saw the bike on the wall of the staff room. We hadn't seen this even though we were in this room daily to get our tools. We only saw it because the last of our volunteer money went on skylights for the roofs – a huge improvement – now the kids and teachers could see. There was no electricity at the school when we were there, it would come some months later.

Between tea-time and lunch I worked close to Godfrey, both sweating to get the job finished, we laughed a lot as I shouted yalla yalla (Arabic for hurry hurry – I think...) to everyone, and shouted 'great job, we can do it, just a few more wheelbarrows...' all were in good spirits. At lunchtime I sat with Bella and she gave me the exact figures, year 1-1000SEK, year 2-600SEK year 3-600SEK year 4-2000SEK (in total 4200SEK that is about 450€). I decided there and then. I would pay for Godfrey's three kids to go to secondary school – he who saves one life... Bella hugged me and said this was a most precious gift to Godfrey... I was so happy.

I asked her to tell him as it's complicated when not talking about building and blocks and cement and 'one more' wheelbarrow. He ran from Bella to me and hugged me with tears in his eyes, 'you are most precious friend, thank you, and may God bless you'. I had told Anne (who had been with us for the entire project) that I was going to do this, but no-one else, so when Godfrey came running she told the others, there was a photo shoot and I felt so embarrassed but very happy. He took his daughter Jacqueline to me and he told her and she hugged me too, so I told her to study well and she would be taken care of, she smiled so wide... a magic moment. Godfrey held my hand a few minutes – it was a really warm moment – a unique thing that all appreciated but Godfrey especially....

At about 2pm we had a closing ceremony, the kids sang for us and we drank coke and ate fruit. Bella thanked all of us for all our work and Louisa was given nice presents, we also sang for the kids, (badly) but fun anyway... after it was all over Godfrey asked for a photo with him and his 2 daughters, Jacqueline and Jessica (12 and 10) - of course it had to happen, another photo shoot... I do have a picture of Thomas (2) also somewhere. We left the school at 3pm, walked to the house, Godfrey beside me all the time, as we packed up our van he kept helping me and all the time he had tears in his eyes, just before I left he said – you saved my children's future, you saved my children's lives and for this – I thank you... we both cried as did many around us... he who saves one life, saves the world entire. It just was so perfectly right... I left with a heavy but warm heart, I had made a difference after all... now back in Moshi, a long hot shower then dinner... I will be back here to see Godfrey and his beautiful kids... this was a very significant moment; you will just have to come along too.... ☺, and see the mess we made....

I look forward to hear your reflections on both this as well as your week and your factory visit from yesterday... also I hope this goes away, with poor Wi-Fi world here just now – you just never know.

I send you many many hugs – see you very soon... XX

Godfrey, his daughters Jessica and Jacqueline and me. This was a great moment, I felt at last I could leave some impression. Godfrey has a beautiful family. Finally, after 29 years of waiting I landed after my 'Leap of faith' and in the best way possible.

Saturday 430pm

I am just after checking what available BoKloks apartments are still available in the same area in Kristianstad and if so if it's possible to change from 81sqm to 53sqm ... will see what they say. I know the 81sqm are easily sold and the 53sqm are not – it may need some extra admin etc. and costs but it would be then solely mine and no need for extra rooms or house mates – thought a lot about it last night... will see what happens, my current apartment is still for sale... hhhmmmm...

One of the completed walkways we had built

Anyway today it was canoeing to Kenya, I survived... it was good fun but got so wet... some people should never be allowed in boats, it took time to get control of the boat but once it was under control it went well, a few good photos to share too.

The motto for today... The government of today is the guy holding that gun... it seemed like it should be a poem later. As we drove to Lake Chala we were stopped by a few guys at a gate and asked to pay 250kr – and if we don't I said, then you answer to the guy with that gun over there. Apparently this type of robbery is quite common, guys dressed in green army type clothes and carrying machetes and guns... time to pay. After we drove away the driver said – the government of today is the guy holding the gun... how right he was...

We got to the lake and ordered lunch then off down to boats and canoeing across to Kenya – it took an eternity to get there but we made it, the other boat did too but they were very inexperienced and nearly knocked my boat over. I found out 10 minutes ago that there were once crocodiles in this lake... if I had known yesterday – and since I cannot swim, this may have been a major incident... anyway, after getting back from Kenya it was time for lunch – the most beautiful chicken salad I ever had – wow... need to buy some spices here... after lunch and a beer it was time to come back to Moshi. There is now a carnival of music and noise as I sit overlooking the street, I like it here. It will be a calm evening as the gang are all tired and so is my pc – need to charge soon...

Saturday 930pm

Just back from Kinderoko hotel, next door, went for shopping and haggling at 1730, some bought some stuff, they know to not argue with me, and that I buy nothing so they ask when my friends will come. Many ask if I will have anything left when I am leaving and if so, if I will trade it against some goods they sell... can't think of anything actually – not just now at least.

Was offered drugs for 3rd time this week... on the streets there are dealers everywhere – did all that 20yrs ago so it doesn't interest me anymore but fun to see these dealers try out to sell... again I don't buy.

Dinner was chicken and rice – there is an obvious trend here they take at least an hour with food as they earn most on drinks and of course we are always thirsty... typical.

I thought a lot about Godfrey today and I hope he feels good and that they had a nice evening at home last night in the new hope I think I may have given... at least I hope he feels that way; I feel happy at least.

I thought continuously about your days and evenings and how you think, and what you think about, I am far too curious to know lots... and want to understand and listen – a lot.

We were told that there is a rainstorm coming so they may turn off all the internets (as they call it) and if so they will let all know at 10pm... will see how much is written then....

So some other stuff now besides the daily news... hope that's ok... some great moments in time...

I was a cyclist when I was younger, I was in a cycling club in my town and had a cool bike called Raleigh Solo, after that I had a Raleigh Eclipse, both racing bikes... In 1985-1988 I cycled a lot and during 1987 I had my greatest moment on a bike – I was 16 so you were 9-10 I guess...

My sister Pauline was working in Cork city in Ireland and I had a close relation to her, so when Easter came in 1987 I decided to cycle to her place, it was 200kms... and I usually cycled 300kms per week so in one day it was well possible. It was a day I will never forget and one of those days that changed everything...

It started at 630am having breakfast with father and he was asking why I wasn't going to work that day so I told him I was cycling to CORK – 'no chance' he said – 'way too far'... of course but what if it was possible, father had never driven 200kms in a day so he didn't get it.

I left at 7am...after the first 15kms it started raining, I really considered turning back, after all it was just 15kms home again, the rain wouldn't stop – all day. After 30kms I was wet all the way through to my skin and I was so cold, should I go home, still ok, to do that, it's just like a normal Sunday rainy day out, just 60kms in the rain. I had the give up devil on one shoulder and Muhammad Alis 'impossible is nothing' on the other – what a team they made. It had a riot in my head and these two characters for company.

Kate worked in Waterford (56kms from home) and I had planned with her to drop in, she laughed at my stupidity to want to cycle further in the rain, so of course I had to go on.

In a town called Dungarvan I saw a signpost 'Cork 100kms', 'Enniscorthy (home town) 100kms' – I was halfway after 3,5 hours – not bad for a wet day.... When I saw that sign there was no turning back, it just had to be done, what followed was the cycle of my life, there were mountains after that town, that I never knew about or noticed while previously passing on buses, and each pedal was heavy. I was (and still am) a big U2 fan, so I sang their full albums for hours, people walking stopped to laugh at me… after 8hrs I reached Pauline's place it was a defining moment in time, I was so dead but I had done it, cycled to Cork… madness to be sure, but I use that day still – just to know that giving up against the odds – not me… that's not gonna happen….

Its 2215 and it feels like an evening to sleep, we lose internet soon as rain starts. I expect you are enjoying evening with Daniela. I will be soon sleeping, after long international canoeing today… and finally a chance to sleep long time… I wish you goodnight, it's another day closer to see you and give you all those saved hugs – I miss you and I hope when we meet we will as able to talk as we can write, 4-5 weeks of stuff to catch up and a lifetime of experiences to share. I look forward very much – many warm cozy hugs – precious you.

Sunday 0750am

Just up, typical when the chance to sleep as long as possible comes, then it doesn't happen… oh well - at least I get to write.

So what will happen with this entire document now, well here is the plan - you have it all just now there is no other written stuff besides this, just adding last night's poem so it's all here too.

What if all the sad songs were right?

What if there was no shelter in the night?

What if dawns release was the end of lonely nights?

What if the evening was when I hold you close?

I dream of moments when all is calm

When a warm embrace takes me home

I dream of a dawn shared

The world outside beyond our care

The sad songs are born from a broken life

From losing love and having tear filled nights

The dawn alone is the breaking of a new day

Like the light of a new love as it sweeps us away

I dream that these days' pass soon

And that holding you close is a shared dream

Embracing the warmth and the truth

Embracing the moment and fantastic you

So there will be 3 packages of notes from all of these writings. From the whole package I will take out the school building stuff and send it to family and some few friends who have wanted to see what's been going on. Then there are the parts that fill up part chapters in 'this Irish life'. Then you have the complete mix with relevance to how I feel and reflections and thoughts of you... I started 'this Irish life' far too often but finally this winter I want it completed and then it will be so, along with book about questions that Sandvik (Global Mining company) proposed I should write - which I want to present to them in November. It will be a busy autumn/winter indeed. In one of the original starts of 'this Irish life' I wrote about concerts that I had remembered and who I had seen. I have been lucky to grow up at a time when U2 grew up and as they became huge so did the music scene and attractiveness of Ireland brought all the stars to Ireland too. We had huge concerts and festivals since my teenage years, when I saw U2 first – in a car-park on the back of a truck in Dublin, they were not even called U2 then and were just noisy. I saw Pink Floyd twice and Roger Waters 3 times, once in the Berlin concert of 1990 when 350,000 people came… it was a few weeks before father died. I saw U2 in 1985, 1987, 1989, 1993, 1997, 2001, 2005, 2009… I like them as you can see. I saw David Bowie with JJ in 1987, Springsteen in 1985, Robbie Williams in 2003, I think… both Live Aid and Live 8 are also outstanding memories. I love the live shows and have paid a lot to see them but U2 shows are most spectacular – an experience more than a show… but that's just how I feel.

So there is something we have to do – go to a big concert, you will see it's something very different… I too have been to a few operas, I treated myself to La Traviata on my birthday a couple of years back in Copenhagen. Was a cool thing for little me to do, was when I was back in Karlskrona for a session soon after and no-one believed me. I liked being taken away by the dreamy landscapes that opera brings, saw Miss Saigon in Malmö also a few years back.

I even saw opera in Vienna once but cannot remember which but the atmosphere was fantastic. On my birthday this year I was at the opera in Florence – very cool too, great city for opera and visit… and hiking too actually now that I think of it.

Sunday 10am – breakfast at Union café – (surprise). I also actually played music – as a kid my mother wanted me to play accordion – I was so very bad, but she thought I was so fantastic so she asked the school once if they would have me play alone on stage during a school concert, I was crap and it showed and no –one clapped – so when on stage now I know I know my stuff before starting, well mostly of the time at least, of course you have to wing it sometimes.

When I lived in Holland in 1993 we lived in the attic of an apartment building Nr 33 Piet Paaltjenstraat in The Hague (don't know why I remember such details), and we worked on 70 day contracts meaning that you worked 70 days straight then had a week off... On Saturdays and Sundays, we had extra staff so we would finish about 12 noon, we started every day at 5am at the glass house, picking roses. Anyway on those days we finished early we would often take the train to Antwerp and go to the Zand bar, it was an Irish pub. We would play bongo drums and guitar and attempt to sing outside there – it was a hippy area so no-one cared but more importantly few paid so we never made much money, but it was a lot of fun.... I don't think U2 worried too much about us upcoming stars.

At last a breakfast with no rushing away and no plan for today at all, it's a bit cool so maybe the plan that was for the swimming pool will not happen, I am fine with that. Some want to go to spice market at end of street – we ate chicken last night with the most fantastic spices... if only I could get that name I could get some and treat you. I look forward to cooking again too, it's been a few weeks of other food and other cooks and various restaurants, and usually some beers/wine also, getting home and cooking and just relaxing with maybe a wine or water and good company – ah yes... I miss that, I miss you.

I dreamt last night of moving and that all my possessions could fit on a 2sqm meter mattress, just like at the volunteer house, if so it would be easy to move at least... I listened to John Lennon's

'Imagine' yesterday when driving through villages and shanty towns, 'the nothing I have is all I can give' a line from a previous poem I wrote, came to mind but now I know I can and have given, sweat, a few drops of blood and some driven leadership so it's far more than nothing...

I sent Kate (my sister) a picture of myself and Godfrey and his 2 girls and told her the story about their school, she was very happy – me too. The café here has bicycle hiring and a gang of tourists just left for a cycle around the city, madness, the traffic is chaotic and the rules 'flexible' so that's not for me, even if cycling was and is a great pastime and exercise... I always liked it but have had my falls also. Once when I was 8 I fell badly and badly cut my hand, I was unable to write at school, so of course I couldn't do homework etc. the problem was that the teacher was my second cousin and she knew that I worked on farms, so my excuse didn't last long especially since the farm work continued even though I couldn't write... we needed the money and of course her view was that I needed the homework too... oh well...

Going off out now into the markets and gangsters trying to make deals, they recognize me and know I will not buy unless it's their best price minus a lot, its great fun – everyone laughs as we chat with the locals, I like it a lot. Some deals are made, most fail but still on good terms, but like I wrote before it's amazing that all the sick mothers of the world seem to be here in Tanzania...

Catch up soon – hope you are enjoying a lazy Sunday, in a week I will be in Sweden and planning my move, having a local breakfast and paying the bills – a lot to do in those few days, I hope the apartment change and sale etc... all go well.... Can't wait to see you and tell you of all these people and adventures... thinking also of next adventure and how it will happen, there is a line for a U2 song called Zooropa – 'let uncertainty be your guiding light' – feel that now – and look forward to all adventures, hope we can share many... many hugs – saved and new warm ones...

Realized just now that this is quite a long letter... the longest I have ever written that's for sure.

This week we will be at the new village and with new people and surely some new experiences, we work in mornings only as it will be too hot according to project manager. On Wednesday there is a Maasai market – look forward to see that too... ok off out to the market – take care – hugs.... again.... ☺ ☺

Nothing at Moshi market just fruit and vegetables – no hats or spices today.

Just wanted to finish off the cycling story to Cork. Cork city is about the same size as Malmö I think. It has a hill called Patricks hill right in the middle of the city. In every cycle race held in Ireland that hill is always included so of course I had to cycle up there too. I arrived in Cork on a Thursday and took Friday off, trained a while on Saturday but on Sunday morning I just had to try the hill. The most famous race in Ireland at that time was the Nissan Classic cycle race and in that the cyclists have to climb the hill 5 times so of course I had to go one better... so 6 times I went up and around the back streets – totally dead after but another well executed day. I stayed in Cork with Pauline for a week and then left her place on Thursday again. The journey home was the opposite in all ways than the journey there, which had taken 8,5hrs in the rain with my heavy wet rucksack. On my way home Pauline took my rucksack so I had just myself on the bike, and what a day. I did the 200kms in less than 5hrs and as I felt I was getting stronger throughout all of the day, I sprinted the last kilometers. Father had been out driving and he saw me coming on the road, I cycled past him, he drove slowly, I race. When I got home and he drove in after me, he hugged me and said for the second time he was proud of me, I was so happy... that evening I cycled about 40km to keep cramps away and relax, it was truly a great day.

When I worked on the farms at this time we had one specific job that I loved, it was called grading potatoes. By using a very mechanical machine and grids, the small potatoes are sorted from the big ones, there are usually 3 different sizes. During the autumn of 1987 the main laborer, Liam, was constantly demanding more and more pay so he got fired for a couple of months, during this time Jim (Kehoe) relied more and more on me to help out during weeks and weekends, I began to become his right hand too. Mother called me that too regarding father when I was younger. Jim's son Patrick was too young to do as I did, so we worked a lot together and alone, I liked that.

One specific day I remember but from a few years earlier he could see I was very cold, we were picking Brussel's sprouts and my fingers were falling off from the frost. He asked me to come into a small calf house and take away all the shit, it was about 1 meter deep. He said it will help from the cold. He also said to not look at it as shit but if I did then try to think that I could become the best guy for shoveling shit in the world, he laughed and left.

I thought about it a lot and even now I have that story in my head, if I am to shovel shit then do it as well as possible, if I am too fix a factory then do it as well as possible – no difference, except for smell maybe. Anyway back to 1987... in the autumn Liam was gone so it fell to me to help Jim and Michael, his brother.

One day I asked Jim what was the record amount of tons of potatoes they had every managed/sorted in a day, it was 60. It seemed like so much in 8hrs, they were strict on records. So one Saturday morning Jim asked if I felt we should try to break the record...I was super flattered as Liam was known as the strong man on the farm and Jim now put me up there with him... so of course I wanted to go for it. We sat down for breakfast at 0730 and planned the day, we would rotate (my idea) which was new for them and we would have to make 8 tons per hour to beat the record by 4 tons, all agreed, we started and measured every hour, 8, 16, 24,5, 34.... The numbers were increasing as we got better and better at rotation and tiredness wasn't an option, at 5pm we had 72 tons, I got double pay and the guys had found out that planning and targets work even when sorting potatoes. Such a day never happened again but they never forgot it at least for the few more years I worked there.

They knew I would go to college and not just work as a farm laborer, we had a great respect for each other. A few years after I left for Sweden I found out that Michael had left farming and Jim had cancer, I drove by the farm a few years ago and it was run down, I was quite sad about that as it was a school for me for those 10 years... a great 10 years.

Just now its 1245pm on July 27th 2014... 20 years ago this minute I arrived in Sweden.... Just a thought... 20 years – never thought that would happen. What a journey it's been – many jobs, many countries and experiences, it's about time I left for another city... can't wait to be closer to you...

Yesterday we went to the Honey Badger lodge where I failed miserably at drums about 10 days ago...it was cloudy and just warm enough for me, I really liked it there. There is a pool and I swam a while, even though I probably look like an octopus being chopped up by a machete when I do try, it's not the most graceful of scenes watching Mr Dempsey attempt to swim.

While there I read a lot of Martin Luther King's book on leadership, I got to the 'I have been to the mountaintop' and the part about 'like all men I would like to live a long life, longevity has its place' – he was such an inspirational man, but so calm in the face of so much oppression. He was shot on April 4th 1968. Bono sang about him in the song Pride and the entire U2 Album 'The Unforgettable Fire' is connected to Martin Luther King.

Here are some lines from his speech on April 3rd

'We've got some difficult days ahead. But it really doesn't matter with me now, because I've been to the mountaintop. And I don't mind. Like anybody, I would like to live - a long life; longevity has its place. But I'm not concerned about that now. I just want to do God's will. And He's allowed me to go up to the mountain. And I've looked over. And I've seen the Promised Land. I may not get there with you. But I want you to know tonight, that we, as a people, will get to the Promised Land. So I'm happy, tonight. I'm not worried about anything. I'm not fearing any man.'

He was shot the following morning: 'early morning April 4, shot rings out in the Memphis sky, free at last, they took your life, they could not take your pride' – U2 – Pride.

A lot to be learned from those who did great things – but a few of his ideas for me were outstanding:

1) execution, if you say you are going to do something then do it with your full conscience self, aware of the difficulties and accepting that you will learn more – execution is very important

2) knowing the dream, what are you actually trying to achieve, is there a bigger picture to grasp? Determine this and follow it relentlessly.

I have many short and long term dreams, here are some of mine from my before Africa adventure.

- *To be the best quality manager in the world*

- *To earn a million € salary the year I am 50*

- *To write and publish a book each 4 years*

- *To travel to a new city or country every birthday*

- *To spend time with great people and friends*

- *To see my Irish family each year*

- *To live well and stay healthy and focused*

To be with someone who shares dreams and adventures and challenges and who is ambitious to join these adventures and understand my dreams... These past few weeks have woken other dreams – hard to define but the execution of the Godfrey episode went really well regarding his children's future – very happy about that. I wonder what my bigger picture will evolve into after these great days in Africa, finally feel like I am coming alive. Something is changing in my head for sure, and its only good.

So many young people come here and dream of changing so much for so many – luckily, with age, we have also logic and understanding and patience – the enthusiasm of youth remains but the maturity of travels, work and experience helps us older ones to see more clearly, I feel at least – it still doesn't help on a daily basis but it can help with a helicopter view and challenge the organizations not functioning here... there will be some great times ahead I am very sure... as well as projects connected to Africa – although just now I don't know what they are or could be, some reflections at home are needed too. So off now to Union café – more later – just got your sms – thanks – happy to be home soon to see and hug you after all these weeks... ☺ ☺.

This dreaming section about Martin Luther King is in my head now again. I read once that when thinking about dreams then it's important to really think in different perspectives, material, spiritual etc... in that same book it said that most goals are set from material needs and therefore seldom become engrained in the psyche of individuals trying to achieve them. So they set up a simple process of goal setting so that most normal common people (searchers) would be able to use it... it was so simple. Start by spending 5 minutes thinking, no writing. Then write your thoughts for 5 minutes, then reflect for 5 minutes with eyes closed and imagine the effect of achieving goals. Few people can think beyond those boundaries... but the few who do actually go from the materialistic goals to the more personal, real, spiritual and probably harder to achieve goals -they (the goals) become something great... very few get there.

I see when I look at my main goal to be the best quality manager in the world, I've been already acknowledged in IKEA, ABB, and many smaller companies as already being that and that's a good feeling but I don't feel it myself, there is more I could do, I know that. The challenges of teaching Black Belts and working with Sandvik globally as well as others, are very much in the forefront of my autumn and winter time planning. A journey I hope to share with you very much.

Its 945am on Sunday – it's so hot now already and we know will not go back to the mountain village (to Godfrey) so this could be the coolest all week, as the Maasai village is out in the desert... according to team leaders.

No real plan for today, was very inspired by Martin Luther King book yesterday and felt like making notes but that then sounded like work and I would prefer to do that when home, today is still Africa mindset. I feel lazy.

Each day brings great opportunities to trade and make bargains and have fun with local business people, all trade everything. They ask me to leave all I can to them to trade so I can get some things to take home, but I have those already and I didn't bring much I don't use. Since I hike then I need most of my gear, I didn't bring too much extra clothes and will wash this week, even though I do have laundry booked for next Sunday in Karlskrona.

It will be a bizarre going back to normal routines and processes after here, as here was so routine in the work and so simple when off. Discover, negotiate, eat at Union, have a few drinks, all before lunchtime – just kidding but the flow when off is very easy/lazy. When you know your way around you just want to actually take a break from it, the noise and traffic chaos and traders. It is nice to just relax and find peace. Sitting at Union (again) – missing music as iPod charges – shite when power is gone at night and the expectation of a nice relaxing music writing period is not realized... so be it.

The guy who brought us to the Maasai village, Dayo, just passed and shook hands – a few know me here especially in the café, I am here most days when I am off, it feels good and I like it. Wonder what it would be like if I were to climb the Kilimanjaro in 2 years from now – if I would remember the faces and they remember mine.

I still think it was a great co-incidence that I found out about this possibility to get here. Since 1985 and Bono's leap of faith it was always on my mind... 2 years ago I spent time in Ireland and started to resurrect the idea once more of doing something... the Irish volunteering companies had simple rules, to work for a year in Africa, I must have a job to go back too, a bank account with at least 1 year of salary in it and a skill that could be utilized practically on a day to day basis in Africa. I never knew or perceived that the setup I actually did use now was possible, so I guess I didn't believe it was possible and now here I am.

After some months of planning and 3 great weeks of work on the verge of project nr 2... a good story. I hope it will be a good week and that there will be a team spirit like the past weeks.

Tuesday 8pm, our last week

It's warm... we left Moshi at 8am and drove to our new village, about 1,5hrs bumpy hours. After unloading the truck, we got to walk through the village and then to the school. The job here is the opposite of last week – its destructive, 4 classrooms needing 4 new floors... one was already torn up and then we started to empty that. After that, we started taking up the floor in another room, very heavy and difficult work, we did that until lunch. Then after lunch we were mixing cement and put down floor in first room – looked good, and we all found our roles fast again, good teamwork and fun.

We sat outside and ate with the local witchdoctor. A funny guy. He has many children and some wives. His favorite wife fed us. The compound where his lives has some cars and machines, many goats and some more conveniences than other people. The toilets were not so much better than the long drop at Godfreys village. They were straw huts with a large hole in the ground, simple. The house walls are made of mud and dried shit, there are goats and cows everywhere. The witchdoctors name is Babo, he is apparently famous in the nearby area and people come from all over to speak with him and het healed. I am happy to not be sick as he may want to treat me... then again it may well cure some stuff who knows.

Breaking the concrete floors with hammers, heavy work, and destructive, compared to be creative with Godfrey

After eating, we walked to the river to wash clothes…. Did some t-shirts. After walk it was relaxing a while and now dinner and a movie… nice to relax.

Wednesday 630am

What a night, after movie it was bed time and that was a challenge. First when sharing a double mosquito net with the bearded hairy guy from Denmark, (Christian) make sure he knows he is to share the net too. Nets are hard enough with just one person. Anyway slept a few hours until it got windy and the door blew open, a bit dramatic but I felt if no-one was out walking then it would be fine… I hadn't counted on the night chicks – and no, before we going getting excited - I don't mean good looking girls, real baby chickens. When sleeping with a net it's important that the net is not in contact with your head as the mosquitos will get you… I knew this from before – however this doesn't seem to apply to chicks.

Four or five times I was picked on and woke with the silhouette view of a chick in my face, an interesting experience, I checked for holes in my head – didn't find any. When I was younger I was often told I had a hole in my head, I never really found any, but after these days and nightly chicks visits there could be a risk.

It was also quite warm at various points during night so twisting and turning also got myself caught up in the spider's web of the net, a busy night not sleeping. Today will be relatively short – we work from 830am-1pm as we will later get motorbikes to the Maasai market. They sell and trade a lot of stuff there so we go for the experience of seeing it rather than anything else… Christian (the great Danish DJ) talks about buying a goat… good for him, I am not good with pets… I hope he enjoys

In the Maasai village the satellite dish was important – the walls of the house are made of shit and dirt – a small contradiction

Since I wrote about religion to you and you answered I was trying yesterday to think about it more. What does/did religion mean to me? I think there is some unearthly force behind some of the great things on the planet, but I also think there is an automatic goodness and kindness born into everyone. Many never get to have this for their base or future as they are destroyed early in life but most are not. I like to think that the leaders of churches are aware of their following and keep contact with them.

I think the Catholic Church fails here a lot. I don't follow any church or religion but have enormous respect for those who do... as it their faith, their beliefs and their entitlement. I also think the community within any church is very strong and the people genuinely believe in various aspects of what the church tells them if not all. I think the

Catholic Church failed in many ways and that the values spoken of each Sunday were not always experienced in the home life that I grew up in.

I saw my father pray beside his bed each night but never knew what he prayed for. My mother would come to our room each night and say 'the prayers' but they felt like chewing gum, same lines, same stories, but no effect, at least on me. I think the church ignored their priest's abuses and their pedophiles and didn't prosecute its 'bad guys' in criminal courts as other institutions have to... it let so many people down, me included. The Irish Catholic Church lost a lot of respect in my view as a result of this.

The sleeping area for myself and the three guys, I slept closest to the door, easy target for the small chickens

I am much simpler than this. I just try to live in a good and simple way, mainly because the complexities of our work make little time for complexities outside of it. I try mostly to be a straight forward and honest guy even though in business there are days when being nice is not a part of the agenda. I still do the honest and candid feedback sessions like Jack Welch preaches about.

I think it will be very interesting to discover these things about you and your views, ideas, interests around religion.

Yesterday Ramadan (spelling questionable) finished here and the mosque was running all night, it drove everyone nuts on Monday night. Today/this night was the first night without it, I would probably have slept well if it wasn't for the chick visit... and the hairy, constantly moving Viking beside me.

Its 655am now and the sun is rising, my first African sunrise, took a couple of weeks to see this – well worth waiting for.

Wednesday 7pm

The most bizarre day yet. Started with work until 1pm, heavy as well as sweaty – everyone busy. Cool. We made a lot of progress with floor smashing and all happy with work so far. During morning there was a discussion about not working Friday, I was the only one against this, out of the we are 8 so that was it. We do our last day tomorrow... it does mean though that Friday is off and Wi-Fi arrives tomorrow evening – nice, get to chat with you... I hope at least, XX

Anyway the plan was to visit Maasai village market – we ended up owning a goat. A long story.

Christian from Denmark wanted all day to buy a goat at the market so off we went. The main reason for doing this was that Jordan had said she would sleep with the goat, this evolved into a very lively and funny debate. We discussed sex with animals with the gang at lunchtime so it was a hot and very funny topic. So we had a target to buy to keep Jordan happy.

When we arrived at the market we realized there was very little, basically nothing to buy, Anne buys some shite necklaces otherwise we decided - lets buy a goat. But before that a beer, happily they had Kilimanjaro beer – we bought all they had. Then on to next pub, far too much whiskey... but local stuff, very like south European perfumed vodka – shite. So off to buy the goat, we arrive at the place and the middleman is drunk so we cut him out immediately... Now it was me and Denis (guide/translator) and Christian, they want 60,000 TSH... hhmmm we agree to pay max 30,000TSH... There was no chance for a deal. They tried all they could – not going to happen.

Off to pub again, more beer but this time a long debate about Tanzania education system with some town/village elders. We discussed what was needed and how it needed a bottom up approach to get going, I didn't like that, as I prefer top down in such cases. A lot to fix here for sure but I realized my approach could be wrong after all it is not my place to push too much here. Anyway far too many beers and then off home – no goat.

We decided that the budget for the goat would be 30,000TSH and when we got back the compound owner (the witchdoctor Babo) who owns the area we stay in, said that the only goats for sale cost 50,000TSH, we got him to 35,000TSH but he would choose and agree on the goat. We found one, and all agreed, Christian handed over the money and that was it. Christian was a goat owner, Jordan was petrified... then we let her off... the whole day just bizarre from all angles... very funny and most memorable.

I thought a lot about religion and after reading what you had written again. There is so much to discover about you and me and how we can find common ground but also where we are not at all agreed and these can be great discussion topics.

It's been hard to really describe these days as we know that tomorrow is the last day...in one way I am so happy that its soon over and I really had a great time, but also there is so much to do here and I feel I fit in... weird.

I find myself partly in a dream and wonder when I wake up, but I wonder if I was asleep and woke up here or if here is the actual dream, so many changes and so much about to happen...a wonderful upcoming time.

Look forward so much to see you soon. XX, many many hugs

Thursday 6pm

The work is over. Tomorrow we are off work. It was for me an emotional day. We had spent just 3 days at the Maasai village and it was very far from the feelings of Godfreys village, we were invited and welcome here too but the atmosphere in the group wasn't as lively as before. The team although small had a better social time in the first town. We played cards and chatted there, here it was movies and complaints about work. It was very heavy work and a bit mind changing, at Godfreys village we were making new things for the kids, even though we had to destroy to do so we could see the completion of work. That didn't happen here, here we had to break up floors, and even though they would be renewed it felt like breaking something... we did a good and efficient job anyway but still different. It was so dirty and dusty, and 40+ heat – never felt that before. Today we had a visit of the immigration gangsters, they are officials as long as they want to be and corrupt profiteers when possible.

First they checked the passports one by one and ask why we are here and where we come from and when do we go home, also how much we earn... so many questions, all fine until he asked me. I didn't tell him about what I earned, he was angry – I am the government – I know – how much do you earn? I asked him, that is not relevant here... then I have no reason to tell you since I earn nothing here either, so I earn nothing. He kept saying 'I am the government and bad things can happen to you here', 'cool – like what?' He couldn't answer. I said I have been here 4 weeks and have met great people so what could possibly be bad in the last 36hrs... he wasn't at all happy but me staying calm calmed him somehow and he just gave us back our stuff... it felt like a weird moment but fine. I thought to tell him what we heard last week that 'the government of today is that man holding a gun' I decided not to.

After they left we were finished our work so we played Frisbee with the kids – great fun, sad in a way though as they have no sense of value as they own nothing so when they do get things they break them as they are of no value to anyone. This is nothing we can teach. We saw also how they fought with each other to throw the Frisbee – you know in Sweden all is so orchestrated with kids, they stand in line, they chat but seldom fight for possession of a ball or whatever. Here we had 3-4 tribes and you could see the fear in some kid's eyes when tackling or trying to get the Frisbee – it was also out of reach for us to deal with such behaviors. At 330pm we were finished and left for Moshi, took 1,5hrs but that's the last bumpy road for a while I hope, look forward to my car again... and smooth roads with no cows or dead dogs etc. They seem to think the gods will remove roadkill... doesn't happen often...

When I thought of you today it was about your normal weekend – what do you like to do... I like getting up early on Saturdays and often I walk 10-12kms before breakfast just to get fresh bread... love treating myself.

Friday – mega early. Last full day in Africa for a while although I know I will be back here at some point. It has been a game changer in many ways, people now speak of reverse culture shock – what happens when we get home and start our 'normal' lives again... I don't know. A piece of me will always be at the school, where we sweated with Godfrey, where we bled for the kids, where we did great things for great people, where we created a great team and lasting memories and smiles for those who were there. Who can forget Anne's Uno outrage, Adams 'you know nuffin' Godfreys 'one mo', his cap, his family, his kind smile and great laugh that just made us laugh more... Godfrey – the legend. I feel aware of the upcoming culture shock risks, I move next week to my most expensive place ever, I live a spoilt life and I have never known poverty like these past weeks... why do I deserve all this when Godfrey's children when we started 4 weeks ago hadn't eaten for 4-days so he needed money earlier... I am proud to help his family and his kids to secondary school, to see that joy on his face was priceless indeed... very happy for that... a lasting memory and impact Soon time for last breakfast at union café... nice with no time pressures...

Rachel and Peder with Maasai school kids

Kids reach for the stars

A few minutes ago I was looking at ticnet.se at potential concerts for during autumn... a few to check out but better to do that together. I also looked at Skåneleden hiking tracks – there is a lot to see so I hope you have some good shoes. I will buy more as I gave Godfrey my original pair last week... will have a look in Kristianstad... new town, new people, new life, so excited and happy to leave Karlskrona after all those years. I cannot remember how many different tracks there were but I can see myself hiking them very often as the tracks look both cool and great fun and I love hiking very much... you will have to join me.

Friday Union café 0915 last day

This morning thoughts went to filling time and space, calendars will soon be filled with work and wonder and new days will start. I was just thinking again of movements and how to build something after Africa. I keep reflecting on Martin Luther King's famous 'I have a dream' speech as well as him speaking of 'the Promised Land' and his belief of a long life having its place whether he was with his people or not – they would get to the Promised Land... I wonder where the current Promised Land is. When I was growing up the Promised Land I thought was where Jerusalem was/is... Israel.

Today's news is full of wars and killing and greed and genocide. Where I am in Africa is just hours from Rwanda where, as all know, genocide ravaged just a few years ago. Where the Promised Land and what is/was the actual promise? I know it may be a religious view etc... but what turns man against man, where does that all come from, what religion preaches this and allows such acts... I am not confused but wondering.

I see the innocence of children playing in school yards in the rainforest or desert villages, where they are so distant from the world we read of... the countries spending time, effort and money on these wars seem to not realize that for all they spend to keep their power their spending could develop nations... but war is more important, finding peace through war seems like such a contradiction... its weighing heavily on my mind this day... what movement could start a real revolution to save lives/develop a nation, even starting with a seed like Godfrey's 3 kids – what could be next?

Godfrey I believe is a good man, he works hard, he loves his 3 kids and he tries to survive in any way he can and will do all needed, a tiny contribution from me changes his plan, relieves certain worries and maybe saves him some years of work so he can have a better life... what more could be done? I sit at union café and my breakfast is a school chair, my spending money today is a week's salary for Godfrey...maybe the reverse culture shock has started... but now the real work begins, at home, at schools, at government buildings, who will act?

I discussed last evening at the 'last supper' what would happen if countries made a mandatory pledge that all capable individuals should before they are 30 experience 3 months of volunteering work in Africa, would it raise awareness and help more? Would it raise too much issues of costs? But what are the real costs of humanity?

When I worked in Holland in 1993 I came back with a view that it was my own private battle to survive the hard life we led there. And it was a real battle, a real life or death battle that was decided in the kitchen of my home... this is a long story. Briefly though – I had a light colorful addiction life in Holland for 9 months as well as some alcohol issues, loved them far too much. When I came back from Holland – I was offered a follow up job with the same company picking fruit in Israel, at the same time I was offered a place at university for a quality degree as well as an office job in a milk production company. All interesting options. I knew that going to Israel would mean more colorful and more distance to 'a good life' even if father's last words to me were 'live before you die'. I was still sure Israel would be problematic. I threw that option in the fire. Then it was between school and work. I was fed up of the system in Ireland – this was before the Celtic tiger – so I threw the job away too, so it was back to school – it was decided that Tuesday morning all alone – quality would be my thing... it was 1993, I was 22.

I studied and worked with improvements ever since. Reaching the top in 2006 with the Master Black Belt title... very pleased with that. I often considered this a great personal achievement as it was in my focus from day 1 as a 6sigma student. To get to the top as best quality manager in the world is a longer and more subjective journey. So when I come back from Africa how then do I connect the processes I know to the cause of Africa rising?

A poem – (maybe just buying time as I think of that question)

In this proud land

They grow up weak

Tortured for their location

A life decided by foreigners

All they have is all they wear

A smile, a hope, but too often tears

Where to go in this jungle of thought?

Where to shine a light

In a tunnel of darkness

Where to make a stand

As all others fall

Where to place a brick

In a weak and broken wall

For all the courage we believe we have

For all the possessions we dream to own

What could be done to share it all?

What seeds of purity and hope could be sown?

I dream for Africa rising

I dream to move the mountain

To deliver for them

Their promised land

In the world of 6sigma teachings we often talk about taking on huge projects, and the risks involved, we discuss 2 main topics in the process of project selection especially for trainee Black Belts. We always want the trainees to feel that their project is welcomed by mgmt. and that the project will have significant effect of the results of the company. We discuss project scoping - the limits of the projects – so that the interfaces and expectations are clear for all involved. We also discuss the purpose of the project and to be sure they are not trying too hard to 'boil the ocean' or to 'solve world hunger'.

These 2 project selection criteria are important, the scope and the size. This all gets me wondering could 6sigma project scope have a limiting effect, what if 6sigma could solve world hunger? We probably shouldn't boil the ocean as its already warming but that's a different project – maybe cooling is a better focus/greater need. Now back to solving world hunger, 6sigma is the most successful improvement methodology in the world ever... so why not apply it here? From what we do on a daily basis how could we improve just a tiny piece to change the direction we are on? What is the iceberg of issues to solve to stop world hunger and make poverty history? There are huge amounts of analysis done – so what stops the co-ordination of a massive package of execution?

Having seen the vastness of the desert, having seen the density of the rainforests, having seen the need for basic human amenities and the smile of the innocence on poverty stricken faces – then what more motivation do we need?

There are solutions, there are basic needs and rights, there are wars fought for injustices around the world but very few are fought for the most innocent of all – the children. Maybe the Promised Land is a myth, maybe it's a real place, and maybe it's a dream, maybe a lost cause – whatever – I want to be a part of this African dream.

Those born to wealth and freedom in what's called the civilized world seldom experience in a lifetime what African children see in just their first few years. There is something so powerful attracting me to do something here – but I don't know what or with who or how... it's a great journey that now begins... Africa rising.

I don't know if there will be more, maybe this is just the opening of the chapters of a new life story, if so then I hope you will be a huge part of what happens next in whatever context I don't know.

I am so happy to share these notes and ideas and lots to see and do and experience together. For all your feedback, thoughts and arguments both for and against these ideas – I thank you, thank you, and thank you again.

I will send when possible today, maybe I will sponsor the Wi-Fi bill so it will be available.

Take care of beautiful you, I can't wait to see you, look forward so very much... It is a wonderful time to be alive, and to share with you.

Saturday 915pm

All flights went well, first to Nairobi, then Amsterdam and now finally Copenhagen. The day started with a heavy head after last night's second 'last supper' for the gang leaving as well as inviting in the next volunteers. Last weekend we had found out about a restaurant with a happy hour between 5-7pm – called Fifi's – great place with good food and nice wine. It was only wine for happy hour... so yesterday we get there at 330pm to be sure of seats and availability of wine... there would be a lot – and even more... we bought eventually 14 bottles and far too many beers. When at the hotel at 11pm it was noisy between us and other party goers, this was not good since we were to leave at 230am with Chris the shop owner and general transport guy...

I woke at 130am and couldn't go back to sleep, not good at all, it would be a long day. At the airport all went very inefficiently as there is so much paperwork for just basically to leave Tanzania, fingerprints etc. I got to Nairobi and hoped to have decent coffee – didn't happen – far to American – colored water... then on to Amsterdam. I watched the film Noah with Russell Crowe – very good – then I watched some safari films, I didn't really sleep and the food and timing were very late so most were hungry when it finally came, a lot of complaints from those around me – I don't ever care, and after being in Africana time for a month then a half hour wait is nothing...

Amsterdam is one of my favorite airports, also one of the first ones I flew to as a kid – far too many years ago. Once there in the shops it was the first wave of reverse culture chock, everyone buying stuff, some very unnecessary stuff. I worked out that Godfrey earned about 70€ per week for 8am-6pm work with only short breaks, I saw speakers for 300€ in the gadget shop, a golden iPhone for 4000€... lunch/dinner cost 23€... maybe I am going mad after all.

When I got your sms today that you were just thinking of me... felt nice. I am thinking of you very often and am so curious about seeing you live and all those chats. I hope that soon after I get home you will come see me in Kristianstad and help me with some simple details - that would be really cool and helpful...

Listening to Pink Floyd's The Wall just now – one of my very favorite albums that really have been around me since 1979. I may have written of this before... sorry if so. There are some really great moments in this album where he feels so devastated and betrayed by the people in his life. First his mother who overprotects him, then his teachers who beat him when he writes poetry in class and all the kids laugh at him, then his wife who leaves him because of his abuses, his manager who hates his drug-abuse also. It's a very destructive album actually when I think of it so being called The Wall is kind of symbolic as he builds his wall around himself to protect himself from these people...

I love to listen to Enigma or Edith Piaf in the mornings if I am at home — especially at weekends, in mornings for work I have a specific iPod playlist — uplifting stuff... have you ever seen the film called 'The Mission' with Jeremy Irons and Robert DeNiro? The soundtrack for that movie is a favorite of mine also and it's a great movie too...

I wonder if Kristianstad will have some specific mood music? I look forward very much to seeing my new Maasai stuff on the walls there... I think I got some great things, hope you will like them too.

We soon land in Copenhagen — its bright still — nice, I am just now very used to darkness at 630pm latest and dawn about 630am to, looking at the map today actually and we were just below the equator, which explains the standard length of day, all year round, I love the variations that seasons bring, even though far too much snow makes the driving heavy. I also have been very used to eating out for the past month as well as having food provided all work days... now it's back to cooking and brightness — yes. Tomorrow will be fresh bread from local bakery and eggs and passion fruit juice... I keep thinking what will be different when I get home, basically if all goes to plan — it will be a short few days before move during week, I will know all details on Monday.

Ok that's it for sure — the notes of Africa from day 1. I thank you for the patience you have shown to read these and am very happy to have shared it all with you. We now know more than before about many many things... great... and loads more to see and do... wonderful.

Take care of beautiful you, many hugs – see you in just a few days, so much to tell you and so much to share.

I cannot wait to see you and in just a few days. I keep wondering what we say to each other as there is so much to start with. I cannot wait to hear your voice and listen to your stories. I love this feeling even though I cannot explain it.

Epilogue

While writing this letter that turned into this book I felt they were a very detailed account of the day's troubles, achievements, feelings, etc. but there was also something else going on. A transformation of sorts and I decided to look at what you have read and take them from some other angles. I had planned that these coming notes become some sort of summary for a few to see but the insights they gave added something deeper I felt. Please excuse any repetitions...

1985 – Live Aid

Having seen Live Aid from start to finish was one of the coolest days in my life – the greatest show on earth and I got to see it along with millions of others. There was a point in the middle of the show when Sir Bob Geldof stops the concert. He was really pissed off as the show was going great but no-one as was paying up, the money wasn't flowing in – so Geldof gets on the TV and demands 'give us the money – don't go to the pub tonight just give us the money, people are dying now' as he punches the table, pure raw Irish 'kick in the door' passion. Since Geldof was the director of the whole day he also made sure to capture specific moments of why we were there – at the point when he stopped the show he played a video which showed a girl 10 minutes from death... everyone cried, it was the clearest message. We could, should and had to do something... her name was Birhan Woldu. Geldof had (has) a band called the Boomtown Rats and a song called 'I don't like Mondays' – the most famous line is ...'and the lesson today is how to die'.... When he sang that he stopped and world held its breath – he made his point very clearly.

My dream was born that day and it took 29 years to make it real, to actually do something about it... taking off from Amsterdam to get to Nairobi was a huge moment, tears in my eyes, warmth in my heart. I wondered what the world be like when I got back and how I would see it so differently afterwards.

Another great show 'Live8' was held in many cities around the world in July of 2005. This amazing show started with U2 and ended with the reunion of Pink Floyd – what a day that was. Again there was a moment for Geldof to sing 'I don't like Mondays' and when he repeated the same stop at the same line it again was a huge moment, I have goose bumps just thinking of it now....'*and the lesson today is how to die*'... during the show he again mentioned that girl Birhan Woldu – because she didn't die, she walked onto that stage in London 20 years after the Live Aid show – because we made that happen... *he who saves one life – saves the world entire...* from the Talmud writings.

Godfrey's wheelbarrow

The man, the legend

Godfrey is 40, give or take a couple of years, we were told, he was our fundi (Swahili for builder) on our project during the summer of 2014. Our project was setup for a small school in Nkwawanga in the Machame region south of Kilimanjaro in Tanzania. Godfrey went to this school when he was a child, he lives about 300m as the crow flies from the school but it takes about 15 minutes to walk the little hills and valleys to get there.

Godfrey is a simple builder trained by other builders and has no formal education at all, he left school well before mandatory 12 and wishes dearly for his children to go to secondary school. He has very little English but a huge heart and a strong lean body. From day 1 for us he was a legend, not in the heroic way but in a real human warm way, he reminded me so much of my own father that it was like going to Africa brought closer to my father. He spoke in a soft way, and always encourage us to help and do more. He also is a good leader and knows what he wants from people and that he needs the team to work together, his soft voice you would just do anything for.

Oval wheels

When I was a kid in Ireland, growing up on a tiny Co Wexford farm, my father had some small tools and a small old grey Massey Ferguson tractor. The most used tools on the farm were a shovel, a fork and a wheelbarrow. These were used every day to clean out the sheds where the cows stood when they were being milked, taking away the cow shit from behind them… We had a manure pile out the back of the cow-house where we put all this shit, it was huge. Each year father would use this to fertilize the land for various crops and complete the circle of recycling… and here is where is gets complicated, growing up in Ireland we had an air filled wheel on our wheelbarrow. A wheelbarrow needs a wheel of course and preferably a round one. Our wheelbarrow in Africa didn't have this, instead it was rather oval and more flat on one side… I remember the old Irish joke about how the man with a puncture was being consoled by a passer-by who said that the guy shouldn't be too upset since the tire was just flat on the bottom… poor consolation. The wheelbarrow had no air filled wheel – it was wooden, wide and useless. Connect this specification to a wet and muddy path between the sand pit and the cement mixing location and guess what? A recipe for inefficiency for sure and we all know someone who hates inefficiency. We were so desperate one evening that we considered car-jacking a wheelbarrow just to steal the wheel. Is there a word for wheelbarrow-jacking? Or taking a wheelbarrow for a joyride and stealing the wheel?

On rainy days it was a mess to push the wheelbarrow and since we lived at altitude in the rainforest it rained a lot and it took time to dry so we were at the mercy of an unforgiving oval wheel trying to push 40-50kgs of sand in a wheelbarrow already weighing 20-

25kgs... After a few days most of us were wondering what form of insane training would be the gym equivalent to what we were doing at the school, no suggestions and we all had gym experience... oh well – just need to invest in a wheelbarrow once home... Godfrey's wheelbarrow – an experience never to be forgotten.

One single 'jambo' was all it took

On the third day (sounds like the start of a religious story) of work in the rainforest village I was feeling down, feeling like I didn't belong here and even wanted to actually go home... felt lost and lonely. I sat outside the house in the rain and tried to imagine what it was like for the kids to eat and live outside with little shelter and comfort. I felt so far from these people and their daily lives as we eat from fine plates and drink fine wines, it was making me feel sick.

Then it happened – a small girl maybe 5-6 years old walked by.... 'jambo' (hello) she says as she saw me sitting on my sheltered step as she walks in the rain... an awakening – I found out later her name was Violet and that her parents had died of HIV... she still smiled... I realized in that moment that she could be a version of Birhan Woldu – I couldn't save Violet but I could do something for her future, I could use this feeling to motivate both myself and the team.... he who saves one life.

Pity and anger

I had 4 weeks in Africa and they had 4 very different feelings. The first week I felt a great pity for what I was seeing, the people, the hardship, the simple difficulties that they had and how they coped and still smiled to us. We had no clue of their daily lives and feelings but I felt such a great pity for them, it was heavy and tough for us too. We had few tools and the work was heavy, I hoped daily my back wouldn't crack with the weights and constant tough work –

but we managed. We also knew we would go home in a few weeks, so too much pity wasn't needed for us... we all missed the showers and toilets though, the basics, we all also missed meat and looked forward to weekend treats, cold beer and nice meaty dinner.

The second week we had learned a lot more from a few people, we heard about the tax issues and the fabric of society that was very weakly woven. The elements we take for granted in our daily lives, running water, schools with electricity, healthcare, gutters on streets... roads... we see these things every day at home and take for granted that someone will fix it, we pay taxes and stuff gets done. Not so in Tanzania. The government corruption leads to just a few percent of aid getting to the right places, we learned first-hand when we were asked to pay extra to the man with the gun – he was in charge that day.

Harmony and change

Week 3 was great and terrible.

We had worked well in our team and we were ahead of all schedules, we would finish early and move to another village. Of course this all felt great until we all realized at the same time that the next time we see Moshi then we would have said goodbye to the gang, the kids etc. but I felt the closest bond to Godfrey. Each day when leaving work, I felt this great well of sadness as the days counted down to when I would finally say goodbye to him. Godfrey the legend. We have laughed daily over and over again at his ways to motivate, his laugh and his simple ways to keep us interested, he worked so hard and for a tiny man he was so very strong, hard to imagine really.

On the day before we were to leave, we had a chance to visit Godfrey at his home and meet all his family. We discussed as well as we could and one issue that we discussed was if his children would go to secondary school. He didn't answer at all. Myself and Louisa noticed how he avoided this question. I decided just then to pay for his kid's secondary school. The next day it rained. Myself and Anne were getting some things back at the house and on our way back to school I told her that I would pay for the kids, she was very happy and thought it was a great idea.

A short while later we told Godfrey and he was so happy, he just lit up, I gave his kids some hope, some idea of a future... when we were leaving the village Godfrey was both sad and happy as was I – I really liked him a lot, and his family was beautiful. Week 4 was very different – a real change – we were at a Maasai village and it was a very different work, going from creating for the kids in the rainforest to destroying old floors in desert like conditions. The heat and dust, the chickens, the goats, kids everywhere, it was really a chaotic place and difficult to grasp. The Maasai kids were different, more aggressive somehow, still nice though.

We slept in a house which had the kitchen at one side and a large room in the other, there was no wall between, so when the women came to make breakfast for us at 6am, I had to go out as the smoke was killing me. I sat out under a tree and wrote a lot to you from there... even if at 6am it was rather dark. The locals couldn't grasp what I was doing playing on my pc and writing a lot, it was a gimmick for them.

We left on Thursday and took Friday off as most of the gang were wanting to do so and we had new resources coming so the coming weeks would be well staffed anyway. I would have liked to stay for the last day but the gang and democracy decided… off back to Moshi.

Religious reflections

What was taught in church? Christianity on its knee's

I grew up in the Catholic Ireland of the 1970's where God-fearing parents took us to mass weekly and made sure we confessed all our terrible sins every Friday as part of school time. Our school was catholic too so all the basics were in place for a good catholic upbringing…. So where did it all go wrong?

I remember once a year St Senan's church (at my side of town) held a week long mission. This included going to mass each day, praying a lot and at both the beginning and end of the week having a colored African priest tell us of the difficulties the church had in Africa and he spoke of how all the money that was collected was needed to establish and build the church up in these poor African nations…

Christianity was they said 'on its knees' begging us 'rich' for help and support. I remember mother being fascinated by this and would preach to us about the poor African children, if we didn't like our food then we should think of those with no food, those poor African children….

And then of course our conscious would tell us to eat – so we did, mother was no great cook but of course did what she could with what she had/knew…

These African priests told many stories about what they had seen and experienced and it fascinated me too, that someone first could travel so far to tell us but also that they had really seen these things, they were very believable.

The poor lost souls of Africa

Africa was lost and only Christianity could save them, we were fed this weekly and through the missions as mentioned before. How was this so, how could so many millions not believe in the bible, we have to rescue them and make them Catholics – it was important for us all. Being young and impressionable then when the famine of Ethiopia was ravaging its people we were told in church to support but that a similar fate would befall us should we not repent, we were so sinful... Lord save us from damnation. Yeah right. What loving God would let this happen? Are these children dying because of our sins? Am I that bad a person?

I guess so, as our religion teachers – Christian Brothers – were dishing out their views to us daily, it was all our fault so we should repent more and more and be sorry for all our sins as they are the cause of death in Ethiopia – I was so guilty I could have started a whole new religion by myself. I just didn't know what to do or why it was my fault... a very confused Irish 13-year-old Catholic in the south of Ireland.

Then up steps a 'Boomtown Rat' – Sir Bob Geldof. A rebel against the church as well as most other stuff that was close to any establishment. His idea and Band Aid was as far as you could get from the churches wishes – but it grabbed the media and hearts and minds of millions during the Christmas period of 1984. Of course the church couldn't ignore this so they threw their support behind it and asked God to help Sir Bob and that it was though the grace of God that Sir Bob was able to do what he did. What a whole lotta crap.

Sir Bob was and is a realist, he knew that the power of the people was not the power of the church, the church was busy building and protecting its fortunes, Sir Bob just wanted to saves lives, simple. Savings souls could wait, lets save lives first. So the church was immediately in the dark as Sir Bob and his merry men and women in Band Aid took up the light and led us from damnation. Since Bono and U2 were also behind Band Aid also then many of the youth of Ireland were directly involved... the lost souls were of little importance compared to lost lives.

Preaching from lost pulpits

The end of the world is coming prepare yourself to meet the Lord.

I was a lost Catholic at an early age, no real religion ever actually and I love seeing the various places of worship around the world, except for one. In 2007 I was in Israel and worked close to the city of Nazareth where according to the bible Jesus was born and lived, going there was an exciting thing for me, Catholic or not.

While there I was driven around by a Jewish guy and he showed me the huge church built over the well where Jesus apparently collected water and played daily, this felt significant and I felt a closeness of something special. It was at that time according to the guide the third largest Catholic Church in the world after St Peter's in Rome and Saint Maria in Barcelona, wow. It was really beautiful. In 2010 I visited Rome and decided to see St Peters. This was for me was the crowning moment for my despise of the Catholic Church.

For far too many years the scandals of the church were going unpunished and the abuses of children by priests, bishops etc. were depleting the church of its dedicated following. All the trials and court cases were still ongoing or fresh in mind as I was in Rome that year. Walking into this fortress of St Peters made me feel sick. It was as if the church had lied for so long about its giving to Africa and all had gone towards the gold of St Peters, I felt sick to my stomach to call myself a Catholic...

The churches here in Tanzania are the life and soul of many communities, people go hungry to give to the church as here also the people believe their contribution will save them... so the churches are great large buildings and fully supported by Rome.

At our project school we had a visit of 3 missionary women from Nebraska – all were there to see the great work being done in Africa and to 'recruit' - we just laughed. God had called them here they said... I wonder if they had his number, and they walked around looking all religious and above us all. They talked to us daily about the work we were doing and how great we were, 'I know' I said one day, 'but why are you here?' no answer – stunned by my direct ways... we all laughed and they realized we were not going to be converted even if they would have liked that too.

They probably told the kids that God had sent us to help – nope, another probable lie. A few days after they had left us we saw one of them at the Ngorongoro crater, I wondered if God had told them to go see the animals too and who paid for their holiday... probably the poor souls of the small African villages and what was the benefit to Nebraska – nothing I am sure... I am sure they enjoyed their holiday – another nail in my Catholic coffin.

What was thought...What I expected

In my years and months awaiting this trip I was building up some ideas around what I expect to see and feel while here. The images that were sold during 1984 stuck in my head, children dying and bodies just left to rot in the scorching sun. I read a lot about Live Aid and watched all the documentaries I could about the situations in Darfur, Nigeria, South Sudan, so many places that are forgotten in our day to day lives and ignored during their few seconds of notice between the normal national news and bloodletting of other 'more interesting' bloody news. I had no clue what I would see. I hoped I would see some glimpse of hope and some promise of the future. I saw so much more. In my first week I felt pity – pity for the hopelessness I felt about doing something significant, the enormity and scale of the projects needed to resolve such a country, torn by HIV and poverty, lacking education, women's rights, basic infrastructures etc. – how large could a problem be? Bloody huge and with limited chance of change in near future. We didn't get involved in any way in local politics but people who are here now and were here 7 yrs ago say nothing has changed, same corruption, same politics etc... I heard a great line when here a while back. The government of today is that man over there with a gun. This was just after being basically robbed at gunpoint in order to get into a local tourist spot...

In my second week the pity turned to anger, we learned more about the locals and their work conditions and ethics, about the lack of coordination of tax collection and how the rich pay less tax than all others, sounds like tax avoidance is not just a European or American thing. This anger cannot evolve into a concrete action unless the government and politicians globally get some concrete activities in place. The problems in many countries are therefore hard to solve since many of the rich are those in power to begin with, so it is in Tanzania and across Africa we are told... a mighty undertaking.

In my third week I found some harmony as I found a way to make a longer term impact on someone's life... Godfrey has 3 children and I enjoyed working with him. Like I wrote before I felt a closeness to him like I did to my own father, so I decided to give him something he dreamed of and was working for – a secondary school education for his kids, all three of them, therefore ensuring some longer lasting effect of my presence here. To put the cost of this into perspective. Godfrey earns about 76-80$ per week for his fulltime hard labor building work. He has 3 kids and a wife to support. He owns 3 cows and about 15 chickens, he sleeps on a bed he made using cowhides as a mattress, he has no door to his bedroom which opens out into the yard where the chickens run and the cows live... he is poor but works very hard. I don't earn as Godfrey, I have a door, I have no cows, chickens or goats, have a car alone that's worth 17 years of Godfrey's income, there is an in-balance in the world. To provide Godfreys 3 children with the secondary education that will give them a more secure future and then it costs about 1/3 of one month's salary for me... for all 3 kids, surely its affordable and so life giving and so easy... it felt so right but also so little... what more could I do... our real work begins when we get home.

There is no way I felt before I left that I would make this contribution, but being here and feeling its worth in the warmth of Godfrey's eyes was enough to prove it was right. I hope it all works as we plan, it will be a lifelong project to follow Jacqueline 12, Jessica 10 and Thomas, now 2.

Dreams and desires

Anything is possible, all you have to do is want it enough – Peter Pan said that, so did Michael Collins. I never knew I could this – I never knew it would ever happen – but the dream was able to come alive after so long - 29 years in the making.

There are other dreams (maybe even desires if I dare to say), of love, life, laughter, joyous times – this dream coming true felt that all other dreams are also now possible. I could find love, I could find life in new ways and places, I could find happiness... I wondered daily about these things as we worked on and on, building, creating, dreaming, and playing cards to pass the time. I day dreamed a lot of you and what daily life around you was/would be like, I wondered what a relationship could be and if we could ever be closer than just friends... I dreamt a lot of meeting you again and communicating through voice rather than 'just' writing.

'We are what we think we are - All that we are arises with our thoughts. With our thoughts, we make the world' – Buddha. When we arrived in Africa we had ideas of making the world better and that we could manage it – we had great visions of leading huge social changes and being a part of some great revolution.... At least we had those ideas. I adapted very well into Moshi and the villages we worked in, it could be because I have travelled a lot and slept in some dodgy hotels etc. and survived, all the time we dreamt of how much more could we do.

One crazy idea we had was to get all students in Europe between ages 18-22 to spend 3 months in Africa, and that this would be a mandatory part of school as it gave such great lift for us... I guess we too were dreaming. We wanted to think of us being there as having an impact – but there is an enormity to the issues, the values, the ways of life, the traditions... so much to change and then we felt to what? What would we change them to, where does it say we are best, better or worse? We are just very different. I saw the movie Robin Hood Prince of thieves many years ago while working in the Isle of Man. There is a line there from Morgan Freeman

(Azeem in the movie) when he was asked by a small kid if God had painted him – and he said no.... but that he had color because Allah loves 'wondrous variety' and this was very evident. God/Allah/Buddha/Abraham whoever is the chosen worshipped icon loves wondrous variety. We were also a part of this, also a part of the wonder... a part of the variety. I think we touched the lives of too few but still some and that was a great thing in itself.

What changed...Us and them – possible pasts

Us and them and after all we are just ordinary men – from the Pink Floyd Dark Side of the Moon album. There was an element of us and them in all the time in Africa, I wanted daily to jump that barrier, at times I didn't want to leave, not leave the school, the village, the city, the idea of a rising Africa. I felt I would or could be a part of lifting it. I loved being there but also loved the idea of coming home to see you, to see who you were, are and will be... the goldmine of opportunities and dreams that await us.

When Bono jumped into the crowd at Wembley at Live Aid it was his Leap of faith, I wanted Africa to be mine and it brought me closer to heaven I am sure. We watched Kilimanjaro from the pub rooftops and felt we were within reach of a great place no man could make... maybe Africa gave me a God after all... I wonder.

They flutter behind us our possible pasts – another Pink Floyd line... (must be under their influence just now) there is a gathering of 'what ifs' in my head, what if I did that or this or met him or her, what if I never had met Susanne and discussed Kebnekaise, maybe I never would have gone to Africa, what if that evening I decided not to check out about volunteering then maybe I would never have gotten the chance ever to do this. What if you hadn't turned up to meet me that evening in TGI Fridays... I wonder if we would ever have seen this book... but here we are... reading it now and all because you said YES. And more and more YES's came after... thank you.

Thank you for being beautiful, charming, loving, warm and kind, a very special person. I can never thank you enough – precious you.

Future history

'Any fool can make history, but it takes a genius to write it'. - Oscar Wilde. In 1993 I lived in Holland and when there I spent a weekend in Paris. I went to see Jim Morrison's grave at Pere Lachaise – I never knew then that both Oscar Wilde and Edith Piaf were also buried there... cool. Interesting to be a fan of three such wildly different people.

The boxer, Muhammad Ali, asked an interviewer once – what is your future history? What he meant was could you say already what would happen? Of course he couldn't but Ali had such a strong view and belief that he was the greatest that he totally convinced himself and others that he was and will always be the greatest. How true he was. What is your future history, could you write it down, express it, dare to dream it even? I wonder what mine is and as I sit here in Africa I wonder if I could dare to dream creating a future with you as a major part of it. Crossing a line, I know, daring to state my inner feelings, 'who dares wins'. I hope you will be a big part of my future and all its great twists and turns.

THE END...or maybe just the beginning...

My precious Patricia – this book would not exist without you. Thought of you daily while in Africa (and every day since). Thank you for all the inspiring sms/mails/notes/chats – and answering the one phone call I made.

I had met Patricia just a few times before I went to Africa. We had exchanged text messages daily for over a month and had met maybe 5 times for dinner and coffee before I left for Africa. We both had interesting backgrounds and complex family stories. We both had excelled in our areas of work. We both had plans to remain single. We had no clue or intention if there would be a relationship or not and that was all fine as I left for Africa. I knew when I left that nothing would be ever the same when I got back. But I didn't know what would be different or how – just that it would be.

In the months that followed Africa, myself and Patricia fell in love, moved in together and got engaged on that trip to Paris that we planned when I was in Africa.

Together with Simba the cat, we live in Lund, South Sweden.

About Madventurer

Madventure International is a social enterprise organization set up to support and raise funds for the MAD (Make A Difference) Foundation. The MAD Foundation is a Registered UK Charity

Once upon a time (in 1998) there was a gap year student from Newcastle upon Tyne called John. Wearing a tweed-jacket (John wanted to teach) and with a rucksack on his back John flew to Ghana, West Africa.

Barely had he stepped off the plane than John fell into a storm drain in Accra and broke his ankle! John's first night of his gap year was spent in an African hospital. But rather than run home to his Mum, John bravely stuck it out and soon found himself in a small Ghanaian village called Shia helping set-up a secondary school.

So impressed were the people of Shia with the Englishman on crutches that they decided to make him a Chief! John was enstooled as Chief Torgbui Mottey I (Pioneering pathfinder through the forest) and was given golden sandals to wear!

The new Chief returned home where he decided he would like more people to have experiences like his in Ghana and to help rural communities with their development work. So John set-up the Mottey African Development Society (MAD) at Newcastle University. A year later he returned to Shia in Ghana to finish the school project with a team of student volunteers. After the project John's little tribe waved goodbye to their new friends and headed off on an adventure of a lifetime across West Africa.

The Madventurer tribe was born. Read more about Madventurer - **http://www.madventurer.com/home.html**

About Kilroy

KILROY is a company specialized in offering products and services tailor made for youth and students. We help students and young people EXPLORE LIFE. Whether it comes to travel the world or education abroad our goal is to fulfil your dreams.

KILROY's history goes all the way back to 1946 and we are proud of our background as a student travel agency.

*Read more about Kilroy at: **http://www.kilroy.net/***

About Volunteer-4-life

After my journey, I made contact with Denis again.

Denis was the liaison between our team and local network of politicians, material suppliers, etc... we met with him often during our time in Tanzania. During 2015 myself and Denis decided to start our own setup with volunteers. I work at the administration end in Sweden and Denis manages on site in Moshi. Our goal with this work is to help benefit the children who cannot to go afford secondary school in and around Moshi. We want all children to have this opportunity.

We created the website www.volunteer-4-life.com and are very interested to build on this cooperation in this direction. If I could at age 43 do a month's volunteering in Africa, then surely there is opportunity and interest for many others, we hope. Maybe the school system will within some years incorporate a month of practical work in Tanzania for all students – who knows.

I look forward very much to hearing from you. Like I wrote, it is now the real journey starts. I hope very much that we meet somewhere along the way.

While editing this work we found hundreds of mistakes and grammatical errors and discovered how poor my English actually was.

Then we thought that no matter what we do to correct it all it will never be fully correct. We decided to go with it as it is. Forgive the long sentences and regular grammatically challenging text. It was just a letter after all, even if a rather long one.

The end *(again)*

You may contact me at:

padraicgd.dempsey@gmail.com

I hope you have enjoyed this book/letter/story as much as I enjoyed writing it.

Printed in Great Britain
by Amazon